Robin Skelton

Spellcraft

A handbook of invocations, blessings, protections, healing spells, binding and bidding.

Illustrations by Brigid Skelton

D0569318

PHOENIX PUBLISHING INC.

PHOENIX PUBLISHING, INC.
Portal Way
P.O. Box 10
Custer, Washington USA 98240

ISBN 0-919345-21-2

Cover photograph: Fraser Day

Printed in the U.S.A.

Contents

Introduction

*"Magic is a joyous exceptional
experience which leads to a sense
of well-being ..."*

Sybil Leek

I am not a professional anthropologist; were I one, I suspect that
this book might cause me to be drummed out of the corps, for much
of what I say runs counter to the beliefs of the majority of anthropologists. I have been studying what I call Verbal Magic off and
on for over twenty years. Unlike the majority of writers who have
explored the so-called "occult" I am not concerned with Ceremonial Magic, the creation of pentacles, the summoning of spirits
and the complicated rituals of witches' covens. Ceremonial magic
is a learned and difficult art, and is concerned with high and mysterious matters. Ceremonial magicians are interested in gaining
knowledge of spiritual powers, in performing rites appropriate to
the different seasons of the year, in experimenting with precognition and exploring the subject of reincarnation. Their practices
are based upon study of ancient wisdom, and owe much to the
theories and rituals of those who have devoted themselves to the
understanding of the Kabbalah, the Hermetic doctrines of the Neo-
Platonists, and the traditions that lie behind alchemy. I am a member of no coven or mystical society, and I am not concerned with
the investigation of methods of divination and prophecy. I am

solely concerned with the making of verbal spells, and with the way in which spells operate by means of the transmission of telepathic energies.

As a consequence of my explorations I have come to the conclusion that the ability to make effective spells is not restricted to a special group of people, but is present to some extent in almost all of us. Spell-making is a skill, and can be learned by anyone with sufficient psychic energy and powers of concentration. Whenever we pray or wish intensely we are verging upon spell-making; we are sending telepathic messages with great energy. For most people, however, these prayers and wishes are only occasionally effective, for while the desire which animates them may be strong, the message itself is often garbled, confused, and self-cancelling. Only by examining the way that effective spells are put together can one learn how to send out a spell—a telepathic message—in the necessary powerful and lucid fasion. In this book, therefore, I have attempted a brief survey of the main varieties of spells and have tried to describe how they are made. First of all I have discussed Invocations and Incantations, as these are types of spell in their own right, as well as techniques used in spell-making. I have then tackled spells intended to protect and bless, and spells intended to control other people by binding them to the will of the spell-maker and bidding them to act in predetermined ways. I have only made passing references to curses, for curses can be as damaging to the maker as to the person cursed, and it is no part of my wish to encourage people to indulge their destructive impulses. I have preferred to continue by discussing love spells and healing spells, two other types in which invocation and incantation are used and which also include elements of binding and bidding. I have then described in more detail than in earlier chapters exactly how spells can be made, and have incorporated in an appendix a collection of twentieth-century spells, explaining the traditions and principles upon which they are based.

The religious beliefs of the spell-maker, the names and characteristics of his gods, do not matter a great deal. As Paracelsus, the doctor and alchemist, wrote in the sixteenth century, it is not belief in religion X or myth Y that is important, it is belief itself:

Whether the object of your faith is real or false, you will nevertheless obtain the same effects. Thus, if I believe in St. Peter's statue as I would have believed in St. Peter himself, I will obtain the same effects that I would have obtained from St. Peter ... Faith, however, produces miracles, and whether it be true or false faith, it will always produce the same wonders.[1]

If you believe intensely that a certain name is a name of power, then, for you, it is. If you make your spell in terms of your sincere belief that there is a god in the tree at the bottom of your garden, then your message will be just as effective as if you wrote it in terms of any other belief. Terminology is less important than energy, intent, and faith. I cannot agree with those anthropologists who, labelling a certain tribe's myths and religious beliefs "primitive" and "absurd," refuse to believe that spells made in terms of those beliefs can be effective. It is not even necessary to have a specific religious faith; the spell-maker may be an agnostic, or even an atheist, as long as he believes in telepathic power and can summon up sufficient emotional energy to send his message.

Paul Huson, a male witch (or warlock), says firmly, "The success of all your spells will depend on just how much of a head of emotional steam you can work up over them."[2] Elsewhere he says:

> ... all magical power is largely dependent on [Faith], whether it be wielded by people calling themselves witches or saints, as the case may be. Whether you cast a spell for the sake of a church, yourself, or anyone else makes not one jot of difference. A spell is a spell, whether it sounds like a prayer or an incantation.
>
> Paracelsus put the matter in a nutshell when he wrote: "Through Faith the Imagination is invigorated and completed, for it really happens that every doubt mars its perfection ..."[3]

There are two points here that command attention. Firstly, the statement that it makes no difference whether the spell is cast for "a church, yourself, or anyone else" is a little sweeping. Huson himself in another passage says that it is unwise to accept money for performing a magical act, as "for some reason ... monetary involvement appears to vitiate the potency of the magic."[4] Indeed

11

spells directed by self-interest are extremely unwise. They frequently fail, almost always misdirect, and are likely to be damaging. The reason for this is fairly obvious. When we make a spell we are using the power of what Huson calls our "deep mind" to send messages to the "deep mind" of another human being, or to send messages (one might call them "vibrations") to other living creatures or even so-called inanimate objects. We may even, if the spell is auto-suggestive, be sending messages to ourselves, asking for the power within us to manifest itself and to enable us to be more efficient in our work or more perceptive in our understanding. If we ask for something which enables us to function better as human beings, then the deep mind will respond positively; if we ask for something which does not directly contribute to our functioning better as human beings, then the deep mind is likely to react negatively, and perhaps even to be torn apart by opposing energies, pointed one way by the command and another by the deep mind itself, which is not sympathetic to the command.

All this presumes that we can describe the deep mind clearly enough to know its tendencies. I believe we can, just as long as we restrict our description to matters concerning our subject. Firstly, the deep mind, the unconscious part of the psyche, has within it impulses towards both creation and destruction. The destructive energy is linked with our natural biological progress towards death; it is, one might say, "of the body." If we direct our power towards the rewarding of the body, towards fleshly appetites, towards self-aggrandizement on the material plane, we strengthen the destructive impulse and at the same time weaken the creative impulse. If, however, we direct our power towards creative ends, if we use it to bless, to heal, to increase the amount of good in the world, then the destructive energy cannot master us, at least until the proper biological time. This is not to say that it is stupid to give ourselves bodily comforts which help us to do our proper work, to live more fully, but that we must be quite certain that we are not doing this to the disadvantage of others. If you find in giving a blessing that you are really simply organizing something to your own advantage, you had better be wary. The intent is all. Those who choose to make curses are invariably cursed themselves. This may not happen immediately, but it does happen eventually. Those who seek power over people for the sake of the pleasure that power gives them are denying the spiritual equality of mankind, are treating fellow human beings as objects, and will certainly destroy themselves. Here one might recall the story of Faust as well as the careers and unhappy endings of many of the black magicians.

How well-versed in magical lore must the efficient spell-maker become? It is, in my view, unnecessary for the spell-maker, as distinct from the practitioner of ceremonial magic, to know the names of all the princes and powers of the spirit world as recorded and expounded in different ways by the ancient writers, for only to the adept who has soaked himself in this lore will the names carry total conviction, and only the adept stands even the remotest chance of controlling the powerful energies that belief in these names is capable of releasing. On the other hand an apprentice spell-maker who attempts to use symbols that have been used many times before in myth, religious ritual, and folk-tale, would be well-advised to check them out before using them too forcefully. There are many instances of spell-makers getting into trouble, becoming psychologically impaired and emotionally disturbed, because they have unwittingly created ambiguous or destructive and even self-destructive messages, being more aware of the power of the words, the energy they can release, than of the precise nature of that power and energy. Such symbols as blood, and bone and knife (or sword) and fire and wind and sea speak potently to the deep mind, but are capable of carrying many implications. In making love spells in particular, if the sexual drive unites with and therefore reinforces the psychic drive, the spell can gain great intensity and can cause more trouble than almost any other save an outright curse. This is not only because of the ease with which images associated with love can also be associated with destruction and death (the orgasm has often been called the "little death" and lovers' hungers have frequently been expressed in terms of bleeding and pierced hearts, wounds, or breathlessness) but also because the complexity of that combination of sexual hunger and deep affection, that combination of animal and spiritual need which we call love, leads to ambiguity in the message. In addition the love-spell that is directed solely towards carnal satisfaction may cause trouble to the spell-maker in reinforcing the destructive, death-directed drive within him rather than the creative one.

The symbols used in spells are often very powerful and can sometimes speak to the deep mind with such intensity that the spell-maker may release more energy than he intends. When this occurs it is tempting to regard the magical power as supernatural, something which possesses a will of its own. But in making spells we are not using supernatural powers but entirely natural ones, those that in the twentieth century we have come to associate with ideas of telepathy and ESP. We are not breaking any rules by using these powers, though if we use them for evil or selfish ends we are obviously behaving badly and courting disaster just as we are if we use our intelligence to cheat or steal or in other ways harm others.

Men and women have been using these powers for as long as we have any knowledge of human society. While many people think of spells as belonging to the Dark Ages, and as being part of some strange and wicked "Witchcraft" or "Sorcery," those who have looked a little farther into the matter realize that spells are no more the property of one tradition than are prayers. This book is written from the viewpoint of no particular cult, and with as little mumbo jumbo as I can contrive. It is written in the conviction that it is high time we paid more attention to the skill of spell-making and began to understand a little better the nature and use of the psychic energies we all possess.

ROBIN SKELTON

What is a Spell?

1

What is a Spell?

*The science and art of causing change
to occur in conformity with the will*

Aleister Crowley

---

*The Science of the Control of the
Secret Forces of Nature*

S. L. MacGregor Mathers

The word "spell" is often used very loosely to mean any kind of magical act intended to have an effect upon the physical world. It has been used to label rituals and ceremonies in which words play only a small part, and a clear distinction is seldom made between spells and charms. I must therefore begin by defining the spell as an act of verbal magic involving the pronunciation of words, as distinct from the charm, which is a physical object, sometimes a written formula, worn as a talisman or amulet. The words "charm" and "spell" have been used to mean the same thing by many writers and magical practitioners in the past, but there's no reason why we should continue this confusion.

If we decide that the spell proper is verbal magic, which involves the actual or mental pronunciation of the words, we must then ask the fundamental question, "What is magic?" This has usually been answered by saying that magic is based upon the belief that words and actions can affect physical reality in a manner which cannot be explained by science, and sometimes in a manner which appears actually to run counter to scientific laws. Thus anyone who causes heavy objects to lift themselves from the ground or fly through the air without the use of physical means must be said to be practising magic, as must anyone who heals a sick person by means of a spell rather than by medication.

I use these two examples deliberately because they present us with two phenomena which have been much discussed and which have been renamed–in order, I assume, to prevent them being labelled as "magical." The first phenomenon is now called psycho-kinesis and is believed to be caused by the exercise of psychic energy; the second is called faith healing and has been explained in terms of auto-suggestion. The patient has been convinced, some-times by a kind of hypnosis, into calling up his own natural re-cuperative powers and healing himself. The history of magic is filled with such instances of relabelling. It has often been politic to suggest that magical power is not magical power at all, but some-thing entirely different with exactly the same characteristics. From the days of Edward the Confessor until the time of Queen Anne, the sovereigns of England with only one or two exceptions were given to healing the King's Evil or scrofula by means of touch, and the success of these healings is attested to in many records. What could well have been called "magic" was made respectable by stating that the King's gift was due to his being a King by Divine Right, and therefore a worker of miracles through the agency of Christian belief. In the so-called Christian era very few people have been wise enough to understand, with Paracelsus, that magical power is the product of belief in itself rather than of belief in any particular god or religion. As a consequence, those who exercised magical power in the name of Christianity were regarded as miracle workers, and those who performed the same feats under apparently different auspices were regarded as subjects of the devil.

During the nineteenth century and the early part of the twen-tieth, as science became more developed, most people grew in-creasingly sceptical about miracles and about all forms of magic. There was a good deal to be sceptical about, for there were as many charlatans in the field of magic as in any other. Explorers discovering the magical customs of tribes in far parts of the world tended to consider them all as instances of either trickery or delusion. It was not logical to believe that a "primitive" shaman could perform feats of healing when supported neither by a belief in Christianity nor any true medical knowledge. Successful spells were regarded as the products of coincidence or as the results of physical causes whose nature had been concealed by the magician. Thus the explorers believed that if a successful spell was accompanied by an anointing, the anointing must have involved true medication. Sometimes it did. The spell-maker was not, after all, trying to prove his magical powers to the explorer, he was trying to get something done, and he would use any means, practical or magical, to get the result he wanted. Sometimes, too, he did use illusions in order to increase his patient's belief in the power being used, for he knew full well that his patients' faith was a great help in making the magical message effective.

In the twentieth century the situation began slowly to change. Laws against witchcraft were repealed. Such movements as Theosophy, Spiritualism, and Christian Science became more generally accepted, and psychic research became so respectable that it was renamed parapsychology. Moreover it was discovered that many of the beliefs of the magicians and spell-makers were far from absurd. The existence of telepathy was scientifically proved. The use of the old "superstitious" lilting songs which milkmaids sang to the cows to increase their milk yield was justified by the discovery that music did indeed increase the flow of milk in cows and even improved the laying habits of hens. The old spells recited to plants to make them grow stronger were supported by the discovery that words and even unstated intentions can have physical effects upon plants, and that a plant will respond negatively to violent thought-patterns and positively to benevolent ones. The doctors discovered that diseases can be self-induced and quickly labelled these diseases "psychosomatic," thus explaining why so many spells of healing begin by "casting out" devils or saying, as Christ said, "Thy sins be forgiven thee."

They then realized that if anxiety could cause disease, then circumstances could easily make someone sick by making them anxious or fearful. This knowledge, used by spell-makers for centuries, was called, among other things, "stress disorder." Increased examination of faith healing led to the medical profession's growing to accept its validity more and more. Doctors in increasing numbers began to use hypnosis in healing, as had the spell-makers of the past. The experience of precognition, which had previously been regarded with suspicion, and even abhorrence, as a gift of prophecy made to the seer by the Devil, was now included along with other clairvoyant matters under the new heading of Extra Sensory Perception—ESP. After the repeal of the laws against witchcraft, a number of witches wrote books and appeared on television and on radio. Indeed, by the 1960's, after centuries of misunderstanding, vilification, and persecution, the practitioner of magic was rehabilitated as a more or less respectable member of society.

Admittedly this new tolerance of magic led to excesses and to perversions. So-called Witchcraft cults sprang up, many of them devoted to "black" or predatory magic rather than the practice of true witchcraft, the Old Religion, based upon love and the worship of life, including joyous celebrations of the glory and mystery of the changing seasons of the year. The recital of the Christian Creed or the Lord's Prayer backwards, which was originally intended to establish the reciter's political opposition to the rule of the Church and what was felt to be its grossly oversimplified vision of the nature of the spiritual world, became an act of rebellion against all notions of morality. The movie makers and television producers leapt on the bandwagon and produced such charming and silly entertainments as the movie *Bell, Book, and Candle* and the television series *Bewitched*, before moving on to indulge in the sensationalism of *The Exorcist*. But in spite of all these follies, it can be said that magical power, under a number of new labels, has now become accepted as a fact by a great number of people in the West. It has never ceased to be accepted in many countries of the East and by the inhabitants of rural areas all over the world.

This brief account of the way in which magical power has been viewed by so-called Western Civilization over the centuries does, I hope, show not only that the practice of magic has always been with us but also that even in the darkest days of witch-burning and the Inquisition, magical power was not only admitted to exist but even admired as long as it was labelled as something else.

Opposition to magic still exists, of course. Many people are nervous about it. They are troubled by memories of stories about black magic; they are disturbed by inaccurate and ignorant newspaper stories which always emphasize the sensational and the melodramatic; they associate all aspects of magic with the politically-inspired picture of witches as evil-mouthed hags riding on broomsticks or lecherous young women indulging in orgies and seducing and destroying handsome young men. They think of the "Black Mass," of blood sacrifices, of Satan in the form of a goat, of skulls and boiled babies and cauldrons containing eye of newt and toe of frog. A more thoughtful kind of opposition to magic as a whole and to the making of spells in particular stems from the belief that it is "anti-scientific," that it is "irrational" and "superstitious" and a product of "primitive" societies, these societies being described as primitive as much because of their belief in magic as because of their pre-Industrial Revolution life-style. Spell-making is, they say, "pagan" or "heathen;" but they fail to realize that the words "pagan" and "heathen" originally meant little more than "rural" – that heathens were dwellers on the heath and pagans people who lived in the country (*pagus*). They also fail to realize that there is a great deal of magic and many spells in Christian ritual, as in the rituals of all societies, and that every time they swear an oath in court, or make their marriage vows, or give some one the finger, they are themselves practising magic.

How did the practice of magic begin? How did man arrive at the making of spells? The answers to these two questions must involve some guesswork, for we cannot be certain of much that happened before written records were made. But it seems likely that man became aware of the effectiveness of psychic energy very early in his career. Certainly anyone living by hunting in a wild country could not help knowing that there is great power in fear and in love. Animals can be hypnotized by fear, and can be driven to fantastic achievements by passion. Moreover man must have discovered quite soon that some people have charisma – are "born leaders" –

21

and have an inexplicable authority. Once man realized that there were mysteries here he sought for the answer. One answer seemed to have to do with the nature of life itself. Some people have a stronger life-power than others and can dominate their fellows. This life-power appears to be at its height when a man is in a state of emotional excitement. His eyes flash, his expression changes, his voice alters; he is transformed.

What is this life-force, though? Where is it to be found? When a man stops breathing he stops living. Therefore a person's "life-force" or "soul," primitive man concluded, is to be found in the breath. (The latin for breath is *spiritus*, and our own word "spirit" derives from it.) Therefore breath has power, and words (which are shaped breath), can "breathe life" into things. Like thoughts, they conjure up pictures of things and emotions and sensations. Indeed, an imagined thing may be quite as vivid to the perceiver as something physically experienced. Consequently we must believe that there is no serious difference between the imagined and the actual; if we accept this, we may be able to alter actual events by changing the way we imagine them. If we feel we may be able to ensure a successful hunting trip by imagining it with a great deal of intensity, it may help if we not only think about it but mimic it. We can make a play of the hunt and each of us can take a part; we can draw it on the walls of our cave, or we can use words to describe it. If we want to do harm to someone we can imagine him sick and help to intensify our vision and our emotions by using a doll which we will call by his name and into which we will stick thorns. If he knows we are doing this, so much the better. We know already how fear can hurt people. If we want rain, then we can make up a dance which will mimic the coming of the rain. We'll take a stone or a piece of wood and name it *Rain* and then give it presents and invite it to come to us in its usual shape. After all, everything that exists is alive in the way that we are. There is nothing that does not have life, so we can treat everything as we would treat another living creature. Since people like gifts, so do the sun and the rain, and so does Life itself, and perhaps also Death. Something takes breath away, and that something must be like everything else we know, a living thing. We will therefore be extremely nice to Death.

This is how it must have happened over a long period, and so magic was born. In some societies the objects used in this sympathetic magic became of over-riding importance. They became not the *equivalents* of (let us say) rain, but *embodiments* of the spirit of rain, to be revered as gods or as holy objects. From this beginning developed the "idols" vilified by the prophets of the Old Testament, the statues of saints in Catholic churches, worshipped with gifts and the lighting of candles, and the "sacred images" to be found in the households of people of many races and creeds. It is this aspect of magic which led to the making of holy pictures, of ikons, and to the building of shrines containing holy relics which were, and are still, considered to have miracle-making powers and to be able to answer prayers. The elaborate movements of the dancers mimicking the events they wished to happen led to other creations. Their costumes and their movements sometimes became the most important part of the magic. So developed the art of dance, and, in a similar fashion, the art of theatre. We can see the consequences today in the ritual dances of many peoples of the world, and in the vestments and ritual gestures of the priests in some Christian churches.

The verbal part of magic developed slightly differently. Firstly, it is obvious that every time a man wants to heal a sick person or have a good day's hunting he cannot get the whole of the community to put on a full-dress performance. Secondly, in every community there is usually one man who has such personal authority and presence that he clearly has some extra "life" in him. Therefore this man will perform magic by himself, and he will do it with words and actions and magical objects. In some societies the verbal part of the spell took on the greatest importance. This may be because the spell-maker, shaman, witch doctor, or whatever could keep the words secret as he could not keep the costume and the objects, and he could therefore hand down his spells exclusively to others similarly gifted, without any difficulty. He became in many societies not only the spell-maker in private practice, but also the leader in communal magic, and the man who knew all the words of all the rituals. He also frequently became the chief story-teller of the tribe, and so we find the beginnings of literature and poetry.

The spell in its proper form survived the development of sophisticated literature mainly in the countryside, where harsh necessity and the apparently wayward behaviour of the natural world made magic essential. It survived, in a mangled form, in children's rhymes and rhyming games. It survived also in the rituals of established religions; many of the prayers and hymns of the Christian churches are spells, in both form and intent. Indeed the only difference between a prayer and a spell is that the prayer is always addressed to a power considered to be external to the speaker and the speaker is always a suppliant, whereas only some spells take this attitude. It is interesting to compare a spell which contains no allusion to a deity with one that does, and to note how little they differ. Here is a Hebridean healing spell used in 1872 in South Uist:

I make for thee
Charm for horses,
Charm for cattle,
Charm for venom
    And for _____

Charm for worm,
Charm for wound,
Charm for ache,
Charm for sinew
    And for displaced bone.

Death to thy pang,
Decay to thy worm,
Fullness to thy flow;
If pained thou art this day,
    Blithe be thou to-morrow.

In name of the King of life,
In name of the Christ of love,
In name of the Spirit Holy,
    Triune of grace.[1]

Here is another of the same place and time; this one is intended to cure the black spaul in cattle:

I have a charm for spaul,
I have a charm for bruising,
I have a charm for festering
    And for corruption.

I have a charm for disease of hip,
I have a charm for disease of haunch,
I have a charm for disease of spells
    And for flux.

If good befell that
May seven times better befall this,
And every complaint that might be thine
    And every ill, beloved.

Bit and sup,
Nibble and gulp,
    If thou wilt live, live;
If thou'lt not live, begone![2]

It is worth noting that the original Gaelic versions of these two spells were both tightly rhymed and metrical. It is also worth noting that the only real difference between the two spells is the use in the first of holy names and the absence of that use in the second. Other spells and charms used in the Hebrides in the last quarter of the nineteenth century made use of the holy names of Columba (*Calum Cille*), Brigit (*Brighde*), Michael (*Mhicheil*), but there are other, non-Christian, references, and the most frequent name to be used is that of the King of Life (*Righ nan dul*) who may or may not be a Christian figure.

In these two spells the difference I have mentioned between the spell and the prayer is easy to see. The spell commands but the prayer begs. The spell-maker asserts that he has power, though it may be through the Name of some greater power; the man praying makes no such assertion, or if he does so he does so without ostentation. Nevertheless, when the Christian sends his prayer with the word, "in the name of the Father and of the Son and of the Holy Ghost, Amen," he is saying, like the spell-maker, "By the power of these names, so be it as I have said." Indeed, the very word "Amen" (so be it) is an indication of the essentially spell-like nature of prayers in many Christian churches.

There are, in the churches, many kinds of prayers, hymns, and spells, and there are many more outside the churches. All of them are neatly patterned, though they are not all in verse. All of them imply the speaker's possession of power, though not all of them assert it. Many of them are usually accompanied by specific rituals, by gestures, by actions, some of which are clearly connected with sympathetic magic, but these acts and these symbols are most frequently felt by the spell-maker rather to be reinforcing devices, and sometimes protective devices, than matters essential to the spell itself. It is not necessary to kneel in order to pray; it is not necessary to have a picture or other image of a person in order to heal them. It is, however, necessary to visualize quite precisely the subject of the spell and the end you have in mind.

There are several kinds of spell, and each kind demands a slightly different approach. One is the *invocation*, in which the spell-maker speaks to whatever he believes and deeply feels to be the ultimate source of his power and calls up that power. The power he calls may differ from spell to spell, in that the "holy name" or "name of power" he uses must be appropriate to the task he wishes the power to perform. Thus it is usually a preparatory spell, a summoning up of power which, once granted, will be used for a particular purpose. The invocation is an important part of all kinds of ceremonial and ritual magic, and is often used by black magicians to harness the darker and more powerful forces in the psyche. Those who attempt an invocation of these darker forces should know that energies once released may not easily be called back, and that the use of spells for personal power, for the love of power itself, invariably results in damage to the speaker. The white invocation, however, can do no harm, for the energies it releases are those of healing and of love. Nevertheless, even in invoking the powers of good, the spell-maker had best be careful, for sometimes the most white powers can cause disruption, and can bring about changes which, while admirable in theory, may be uncomfortable in fact.

Another kind of spell is the *incantation*, which differs from the invocation in that it is usually not so much concerned with calling up powers as with intensifying existing emotions. Incantations are ways of putting oneself and one's companions into desired states of mind. They are not intended to alter the physical universe, but to prepare the mind and the psyche to reach a required level of feeling and receptivity.

One of the most difficult spells is what I call the *bidding spell*, in which the spell-maker commands a certain happening to occur without the cooperation of those involved in the happening. Spells to summon friends to one's door or lovers to one's bed, to send strangers or enemies away, to alter the minds of politicians, to change the weather—all these are bidding spells. Because no cooperation from the subject is likely, they are obliged to be spells of great power, and are therefore dangerous. They can encounter opposition, and, because they are not made with the cooperation of the subject, they may be dangerously close to expressions of the spell-maker's wish to possess power for its own sake. If they are thus tainted they are likely to damage the spell-maker. It is not always easy to be certain of your own intentions, so if there is any doubt at all in your mind about the spell's purity of intent it is best to leave the whole matter alone.

The *curse* is, of course, the most dangerous kind of spell to tackle, for it requires the unleashing of dark and destructive forces within oneself, and as I have already said, this is invariably unwise. Nevertheless, if a curse is necessary and if it is being made with an entirely unselfish intent, perhaps to defend or protect another person, perhaps to avoid a tragic happening, it need not be destructive to the spell-maker, especially if he perceives that there is a way to gain the required end by means of a spell which, while operating to the material disadvantage of the subject, also operates to his psychological and psychic well-being. This is, of course, to curse by blessing. One might attempt to give a miser the blessing of generosity rather than curse him with the withering of his limbs, or one might bless a cruel man with the gift of kindness.

Blessings cannot damage the spell-maker. They are usually fairly general in intent and aim at bringing peace of mind and health to the subject. They are sometimes more difficult to make than spells with more specific ends, because it is hard to develop the necessary passionate concentration upon a vague and diffuse feeling.

Graces differ from blessings only slightly. Graces are only spells in that an offer of praise and thanks to any form of life is to enhance the health and vitality of that form of life. Grace before eating is not simply a ritual; it is an enrichment of the meal. Grace after meat improves the digestion. The spell-maker, however, unlike the usual grace-sayer, will himself bless the meal through the power that is given him and that works through him, rather than *ask* a blessing. The spell-maker is the one who firmly believes that he has been given the power to bless and must, perforce, make use of it.

Love spells have been much in demand over the centuries, and many spell-makers in eastern countries have these as the greater part of their stock in trade. They are often accompanied by the use of potions and love philtres which are supposed to have aphrodisiac properties, though most doctors are agreed that as yet no true aphrodisiac has been discovered and the effect of these potions is entirely psychological. Consequently love potions are usually ineffective; they may give the donor confidence, but they fail to affect the recipient. Gifts, however, are often effective as accompaniments of the spell, especially if the spell has been made with the gift in mind. Love spells are difficult to perform success-fully because self-interest is usually very much involved, and therefore the message frequently fails. On the other hand love spells which are entirely unselfish, or bidding spells which call up a lover, are usually successful.

Healing spells and charms are the most widely-used forms of spell. These are not in themselves difficult to make, but they are sometimes difficult to direct accurately. The spell-maker may be misinformed. He is not always a good diagnostician and he may attempt to heal a minor disorder which is in fact the consequence of a more serious one. I know one case where the spell-maker had no difficulty in curing a case of rectal bleeding but was not competent to understand the cause of the bleeding, so that the patient had, in the end, to resort to surgery. When the disorder is clear from the symptoms the spell-maker is usually fairly efficient. Skin disorders are easy to heal, for example, and so are muscular sprains. In this kind of spell the spell-maker most usually does little but ask the subject's own body to heal itself. The body is obviously likely to cooperate if the subject is not neurotically insistent upon retaining the illness. If the subject is neurotic, the healing spell has to take on the force of the bidding spell; this can be a very exhausting business.

In all these instances it is clear that the spell-maker is engaged in practices which differ very little from those of prayers. The difference lies, indeed, more in the attitude towards the sources of power than in the intent of the practice. It may differ also, however, in another respect. Many prayers are now said by rote and they are given little intensity, little true conviction, by their speakers. Indeed, I suspect that when prayers are made with passion, when they are made with intensity, the one praying feels that power has been given him and that he can, he must, command it to the good end he desires. At that point, he becomes a maker of spells. He employs the technique of the spell-maker and releases and directs energies latent within his mind, as man has done for thousands of years.

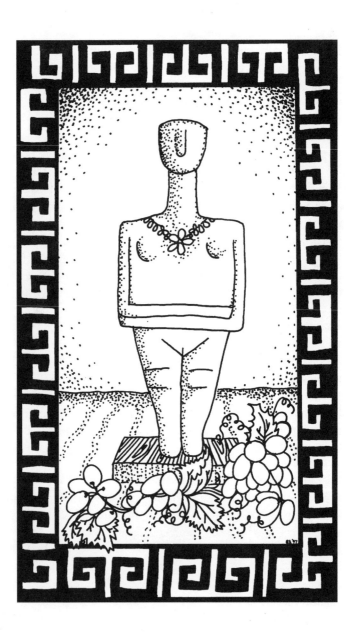

2

Invocations

*The base of all forms of magic however
or by whomever used must be the same
fundamentally, and that base is Mind.
Mind is the instrument, the channel
and perhaps in some cases the creator
of the forces which produce "magical" results.*

Justine Glass

The first spell to consider is the *invocation*. This is in some ways one of the most difficult of all spells, for the maker-speaker must first of all be absolutely certain what power he is addressing. This has less to do with the name, or names, used than might generally be supposed. An invocation addressed to "God" can be, in actuality, addressed to many kinds of power, for the word "God" does not limit the word of power in any precise manner. Therefore it is the responsibility of the invocation-maker to concentrate upon the qualities which are to be contained and released by that "God" word. If the invocation is to have any potency at all, nothing within it must either obviously or by implication oppose the qualities which are those of the "God." There must be complete agreement between the qualities of the "God" addressed and the powers desired. This may be illustrated by the opening of Milton's *Paradise Lost*, in which the poet asks for inspiration, calling in an invocation for powers of poetry which will be used to serve and worship the "God" addressed.

A similar agreement between the power invoked and the request made can be observed in many invocations addressed to gods or spirits which are presumed to have control or power over specific areas of human endeavour. Thus one addresses St. Anthony if one wishes to find a lost object, one addresses St. Christopher if one wishes to travel without difficulty, and one addresses (or addressed) Venus Aphrodite if one wishes to have success in love.

To many this may seem to be the rankest superstition, and yet it is all quite reasonable, for in addressing Saints Anthony or Christopher or Venus Aphrodite one is merely asking one's psyche to employ those faculties which are associated with those names. It is not a matter of indulging in some pagan belief, simply of making messages to oneself precise by using a particular set of labels.

Here we arrive at one theory or explanation of the nature of the spell. It is a way of sending a message. It is an instruction which is transmitted in a code that the psyche (one's own or another's) understands. Therefore it makes no essential difference if one invokes the Muse or the Holy Ghost, as long as to the speaker both these names have the same import. It does, however, make a difference if the spirit invoked is that of Baal or Satan, for unless the person making the invocation wholly believes these names to represent good and non-destructive forces he is liable to release energies which are destructive and evil.

The invocation is usually a preparatory or introductory spell or part of a spell, intended to give the speaker power to perform other acts. The nature of the spirit called upon must be appropriate to those acts, or the deep mind of the spell-maker will not respond correctly and the spell may fail. According to Aleister Crowley the recipe for the effective invocation-maker is, "Enflame thyself in praying." That is to say that the spell should heighten the awareness of the spell-maker, and increase his psychic energy to such an extent that the following spell can be made with the maximum emotional power. The spell-maker must not only consider whether or not the name he uses is appropriate intellectually to the task he intends, but also how that name affects him emotionally. He must pick a name that *feels* right as well as one that he *thinks* is right.

Acts performed in one name will differ fundamentally from those performed in another, even if those acts appear to be entirely the same. Thus the bidding spell to call a loved one to one's door, if performed in the name of Satan, will differ in its effects from a bidding spell with superficially the same intention made in the name of the Muse or the Goddess of Love. In invocations, as in all spells, we are dealing not with labels but with the energies released by those labels. To make a parallel: the money given to the poor from love and pity is good, without doubt; the money given to the poor in order to enslave them is undoubtedly bad. The immediate effect is the same, but the consequences follow the intent, not the fact. In the making of invocations, as in the making of all spells, the intent is all.

Many people who have made use of the divinatory wisdom of the *I Ching* have discovered that when they have cast their coins or yarrow stalks, the ideogram that the *I Ching* presents is the answer not to the question ostensibly put but to the question actually asked. One may ask "What is to become of my marriage?" or "What should I do next?", when one means "What should I do about my anxiety problem?" The answer, in the case of the *I Ching*, applies always to the actual, as distinct from the ostensible, question.

As with the *I Ching*, so it is with spells. Because the spell-maker can easily delude himself into believing that the name used in the invocation has certain wholly good attributes, while in fact it is serving as a vessel for attributes which are not wholly good, it is necessary to be especially careful in the making of invocations. It is so easy to address, ostensibly, Love, while actually addressing Greed or Lust. It is so easy to believe that one is calling upon Justice when one is really calling upon Prejudice or Envy. It is not always easy for the maker of spells to disentangle one intent, or feeling, from another. It is here, of course, that ritual helps. The spell-maker who feels able to make wholehearted use of an established ritual, whether of Witchcraft or of another religion, is protected from making mistakes. The ritual is objective and its intent is fully defined, so if the spell-maker unconsciously intends something other than that intended by the ritual the spell will fail.

33

There is, of course, no way to convince anyone of the power of invocations unless they wish so to be convinced. I could quote example after example of invocations which have "worked" and command no belief whatsoever. I can only, without any wish to be superficial or specious, point to the many invocations to the Muse to be found at the commencement of poems, and suggest that not all of these are entirely conventional gestures. Power was asked for, and power was received.

It is the nature of this power which causes many to remain dubious of the whole procedure. What power is it? How does it feel to the "possessor" of it? Is there any physical sensation which accompanies it and testifies to its presence? Few people have commented upon this power, but those who have done so have pointed to an actual physical effect. This is certainly the case with so-called "creative inspiration" and seems also to be the case with "religious" inspiration (and here one must recognize the word "inspiration" itself as a word suggesting the possession of a person by a "spirit" or "power").

In the beginning the invocation-maker feels a sense that communication with the source of power, with the God or Muse or Spirit, is possible. This sense of the possible is hard to describe. It is partly a feeling of awareness, a tense anticipation of the kind one has when believing, but not exactly knowing, that the phone may ring and a longed-for voice will be heard. It is a feeling of restlessness and yet of growing certainty. As the invocation begins, the doubts and nervousness fade and are replaced by a feeling of confidence and joy and the words arrive with less and less conscious thought and, usually, ever more quickly. It is as if the spirit addressed were accepting the invocation even while it is being made, for it seems as if the power is itself dictating the words which are invoking it. As the invocation continues it is not unusual for the speaker to become physically affected. The body temperature rises; sometimes there is a nervous prickling at the roots of the hair, especially at the nape of the neck; the eyes become unfocused and stare "through" rather than "at" what is before them. Sometimes the breathing rate changes, and the speaker finds that he is

34

taking deeper breaths, almost gulping the air as if it were feeding him with ever-increasing amounts of power. As the invocation closes the maker is confident of being able to proceed with the next stage of the action and make the request he has in mind, or perform the spell he now has the power for, or simply go ahead with whatever non-magical work it is for which he has asked help.

The physical aspect of the maker in the state of "trance" which accompanies the making of an invocation and attends its apparent success has been noted many times. We have records of magicians changing colour, sometimes falling into pseudo-epileptic fits, sometimes suddenly leaping higher or in a more contorted manner than seems possible to a body unaided by special powers. We also have records of poets and musicians at times of inspiration becoming very much changed in appearance. Schubert, when inspired, spoke in an altered voice and his acquaintances speak of his eyes "flashing." Wagner's features became very much changed and he looked like a wild man. Beethoven's eyes rolled and flashed or stared immovably, the pupils often rolled upward.

It is by no means certain whether these physical changes are caused by the presence of power, or whether they are physical means towards the gaining of power. Many spell-makers quite deliberately alter their body movements and their facial expressions when at work, changing the normal attitudes of the body so that sheer physical habit cannot inhibit new perceptions. Some, of course, prevent the inhibiting influence of normal mental and emotional habits by adopting a special form of dress, or by wearing rings, necklaces, or pendants of a kind that seems to be appropriate.

In societies which still practise a form of magic in which the verbal spell and the physical rituals and costumes are still in absolute unity, the invocation-maker has special clothing to wear and special magical objects to assist him. In these societies it is often felt that the ritual is more important than the verbal spell, and the spell itself may be rudimentary. This is the case in many magical rituals of West Africa. In other societies, such as those of Melanesia, the spell itself is regarded as being of primary importance. In these societies the physical accompaniments of the verbal spell tend to be regarded as reinforcing and safeguarding the direction of the spell rather than as being absolutely essential to it.

In cases where words do form a part of a magical act, and certainly in all cases where the magical act itself is wholly verbal, great attention is paid to the voice of the spell-maker or spell-performer. N. K. Chadwick says in *Poetry and Prophecy*, "in the *Rhorfinns Saga Karlsefnis* the seeress who is called in to give an oracle insists that she cannot get the spirits to attend to her until she can get a *singer with a good voice* to chant the required spells" and later says, "The spirits come in definite response to words and music, and no other compelling power is needed."[1]

The invocation is often a beginning, and it leads towards other acts. It differs from the incantation only in that the invocation must be addressed to a power considered to be, or treated as being, external to the speaker, whereas the incantation does not necessarily have this limitation. Nevertheless the style of the invocation is most frequently incantatory, and by the word incantatory I mean not only that it is in the form of a chant or song (Lat. *cantare*: to sing), but that it proceeds by cumulation and repetition rather than by logical or narrative stages.

The way in which the invocation relates to the succeeding magical acts is well shown by the *kaylavala dabana taytu* spell of the Trobriand islanders. This spell is made to increase the growth of the mop-like head of the *taytu*. The millipede is invoked as the embodiment of speedy movement and also, Malinowski suggests, as a spirit of fertility because it is a "prognostic of downpour."

I
"Millipede here now, millipede here ever!
Millipede of the promontory of Kabulukwaywaya, shoot
along, shoot along, shoot along to Kabulukwaywaya, shoot along
as far as Dulata. Millipede of Dulata, shoot along, shoot along,
Shoot along to Dulata, shoot along and shoot along back to
Kabulukwaywaya. Millipede shoot along.

II

"The millipede shoots along, shoots along.
Thy head, O *taytu*, shoots along as the millipede shoots along,
Thy leaves, O *taytu*, shoot along as the millipede shoots along.
Thy forks, O *taytu*, shoot along as the millipede shoots along.
Thy secondary stalks, O *taytu*, shoot along as the millipede
    shoots along.
Thy shoots, O *taytu*, shoot along as the millipede shoots along.
Thy overground roots, O *taytu*, shoot along as the millipede
    shoots along.
Thy aerial root, O *taytu*, shoots along as the millipede shoots
    along.

III

"Shoot up, O head of my *taytu*,
Heap up, O head of my *taytu*.
Make mop upon mop of leaves, O head of my *taytu*.
Heap together, O head of my *taytu*.
Gather up, O head of my *taytu*.
Make thyself thick as the *yokulukwala* creeper, O head of my
    taytu."[2]

Only the first part of this spell is invocation; the second and third
parts are clearly bidding spells. In this spell as in the many of the
spells of the Trobriand Islanders the invocation begins with the
request for the power to come "here." Other spells begin "Spider,
here now!" and "Full moon here! Full moon then, full moon here
ever." The Trobriand islanders make a distinction between spells
which are accompanied by rituals, as are all the spells I have
referred to so far, and spells which are called *megwa wala o wadola*,
which means "magic just of mouth," and which have no ritual
attached to them. An interesting spell which reveals very clearly the
incantatory, and indeed hortatory, element in the spell is the
vasakapu sobala which invokes the power of the quickly growing
Dadeda plant in order to make the sprouts of the *taytu* plant come
out (*vasakapu sobala* means "to make come out"):

37

I

"Come out, come out, come out, come out.
Come out, come out anew, come out, come out.
Come out of old, come out, come out.
Come out in the evening, come out, come out.
Come out at noon, come out, come out.
Come out at daybreak, come out, come out.
Come out in the morning, come out, come out.
O *dadeda* tree that comes out, comes through.

II

"O *dadeda* tree that comes out, comes through.
O old skin, come out, O *dadeda* tree that comes out, come
    through.
O slow-sprouting *imkwitala taytu*, come out, O *dadeda* tree
    that comes out, comes through.
O slow-sprouting *katumyogila taytu*, come out, O *dadeda* tree
    that comes out, comes through.
O *taboulo taytu* with the rotten patch on it, come out, O *dadeda*
    tree that comes out, comes through.
O rotten *taytu*, come out, O *dadeda* tree that comes out, comes
    through.
O blighted *taytu*, come out, O *dadeda* tree that comes out,
    comes through.
O *tirimwamwa'u taytu* of the heavy growth, come out, O
    dadeda tree that comes out, comes through.

III

"Thy shoots are as quick as the eyes of the *kapapita*, the quick
    bird.
Thy shoots are as quick as the *kababasi'a*, the quick black ants.
Thy shoots are as quick as the *ginausi*, the quick thing.
Shoot up, shoot up, shoot up, O *taytu*."[3]

In a society as highly organized in terms of its ritual and its
magical practices as that of the Trobriand islanders, it is obvious
that the spells, particularly the invocatory parts, are part of a well-
founded and long-standing orthodoxy. It seems clear also that no

doubts as to the efficacy of the magic have been planted by the proponents of alternative religio-magical beliefs. This state of affairs is unusual. In most countries of the world orthodox religion is practised alongside magic, and the magical formulae are frequently altered under the pressure of the local orthodoxy, except in the case of Hinduism, which has such a capacity for containing within it almost all possible religious and magical beliefs that the spells of Hindu India do not seem to have been very much altered. In some cases the spell-maker, confused as to exactly which power is the most effective, contrives to combine names from *different* ortho-doxies, and sometimes in a fashion which appears to be inappro-priate, as the Malaysian spell which opens with a fine attempt to hedge all bets by invoking the power not only of Allah but also of Iblis (Satan):

In the name of Allah, the Merciful, the Compassionate.
Friend of mine, Iblis! and all ye spirits and devils
Who love to trouble man,
I ask you to go and enter the body of this girl,
Burning her as this sand burns,
Fired with love for me.
Bring her to yield herself to me!
By virtue of this rice and steam
Place her here by my hearth
Or else take ye heed![4]

Admittedly here Allah is invoked as the main power, but still the whole spell is not only "patently impious" but also curiously impertinent.

A similar bringing together of names whose powers might be thought to stem from two different beliefs, or two different ortho-doxies, can be seen in some of the spells of the Hebrides, as in the following charm to cure "red water" in a cow. The spell itself follows an act of sympathetic magic. Alexander Carmichael tells us that:

In making the incantation of the red water, the exorcist forms her two palms into a basin. She places this basin under the urine

39

of the cow or other animal affected, and throws the urine into water, preferably running water, to carry away the demon of the complaint. Having washed her hands in clean cold water, the woman forms them into a trumpet. She then faces the rising sun, and intones the incantation through the trumpet as loudly as she can.

> In name of the Father of love,
> In name of the Son of Sorrow,
> In name of the Sacred Spirit,
>   Amen.

> Great wave, red wave,
> Strength of sea, strength of ocean,
> The nine wells of Mac-Lir,
> Help on thee to pour,
> Put stop to thy blood,
> Put flood to thy urine.
>   (*The name*)[5]

Mac-Lir means, literally, "Son of the Sea" and is a sea god. The spell implies that the exorcist has equal faith in two theologies. This kind of fusion is not uncommon, though some societies, or perhaps I should say some members of some societies, appear to have no difficulty in identifying the right power to invoke. A spell of the Creek Indians of Alabama opens with a very simple and authoritative invocation:

> O, spirit of the white fox, come.
> O, spirit of the white fox, come.
> O, spirit of the white fox, come.
> O, hater of snakes, come.
> Snakes who have hurt this man, come.
> Come, O white fox, and kill this snake.[6]

Succeeding stanzas follow the same form exactly, and only one word changes in each stanza. The second stanza calls for the "red fox" and the third and final stanza for the "black fox." This spell reveals both the repetitive nature of the invocation and its frequent use of a cumulative progression. White is followed by red is followed by black; black is the climax and, I suggest, the most powerful of the colours in this particular context, as it is a colour commonly associated with ideas of night and death. Moreover it is interesting to note here that the invocation takes up the greater part of the spell, whereas in other spells we have examined it often takes up only the opening two or three lines. In other cases the element of invocation does not enter the poem or spell until the nature of the demand is clear. An entertaining small spell of the Yoruba of West Africa illustrates this pattern perfectly:

Song: Pay me a visit!
            Pay me a visit!
            O Money, pay me a visit!
            I'm living in this town.
Refrain: Pay me a visit![7]

This spell shows us that invocations may also be summoning spells and bidding spells without losing their invocatory character. The difference between the invocation proper and the summoning spell is that in the summoning spell the speaker assumes power over that which he is summoning, while in the invocation it is clear that the power is being mustered in the name of that which is being summoned.

In these times it is not easy for most spell-makers to invoke powers without very careful thought, for the general development of forms of monotheism in most parts of the world has deprived us of any easy means of naming appropriate powers for particular interests. We may, if we are Catholics, or even if we are convinced that the names of some Catholic saints of the Catholic church define the message which we wish to construct with some degree of accuracy, use the names of saints. In many instances, however, we cannot identify the appropriate powers readily, and ready identification is important, for it means that we can immediately associate certain qualities with certain names. Unlike the Trobriand Islanders, we have no set vocabulary to work with. Unlike the Hebridean spell-makers and exorcists, we have only an academic understanding of folk-wisdom and folklore, and most of us cannot feel wholeheartedly bound up in the customs and traditions of even our grandfathers. Out of touch with the natural rhythms of the countryside which furnish words of power that speak more directly and forcefully to the psyche than words which do not refer to age-old and natural sequences of events, we sit in concrete boxes and get so out of touch with the fundamentals of life that we are obliged to rush to psychiatrists. It is perhaps best, in these circumstances, not to attempt to invoke a power in the form of a named person or creature, but to invoke, more abstractly, the spirit which embodies the quality you are seeking to employ. Thus one might begin an invocation

> Spirit of Peace, come to me
> Spirit of Peace, come to me
> Spirit of Peace, come to me

concentrating all the time upon the feeling of peace, upon the precise mood of peace that is desired. In this, however, as in all acts of verbal magic, all *megwa wala o wadola*, it is essential to be most precise in language and attitude, or the message coded to the psyche will be misread or unintelligible and the spell will fail.

This precision is the more difficult to achieve because in the making of the spell, either by writing it down or by creating it orally, there must be no hesitations, no second thoughts, for such pauses break the concentration of the spell and therefore its power. The spell must be created without interruption if it is to be effective. There is one exception to this rule. It is possible to write a spell with care, making many revisions, if the writing is not to be the actual act of transmission. Once the spell is completed it must then be spoken, either aloud or in the mind only, with absolute concentration and intensity, all earlier hesitations and refinings forgotten. In these cases it is wise to speak it, to transmit it not once but several times, the favoured number being three, for that provides the most obvious and simple form of cumulative intensification. This repetition, or rather re-creation, of a spell calls for great concentration. This is especially the case if the spell is one composed by somebody else; the traditional spells which have been handed down from generation to generation may prove to be entirely ineffective if they are treated perfunctorily or if the speaker, in the saying of them, does not fully "experience" them. In some societies the traditional messages are held in such wholehearted reverence that it is not too difficult to make use of them; but in others they have lost their power because they have become over-familiar. Anyone who has ever attempted to use well-known prayers with real intensity of feeling knows that this is a difficult thing to do. In some societies this difficulty is recognized and an attempt to solve the problem is made by requiring the praying or worshipping person to repeat the prayer not three times only but over and over again. These repetitions, because ultimately mindless, may be effective in that though they lack passion, they are not weakened by any intrusive activity of the person repeating them, and therefore whatever virtue lies in the words themselves may be made operative by sheer cumulation. In countries where prayer wheels are used, the operator of the prayer may not even be sure what prayers are being repeated. Catholics make a not dissimilar use of holy beads, and in other societies other means are used to present prayers and spells without requiring actual magical concentration from any-body.

This is one solution to the problem of familiarity. The other is, of course, to prevent the material becoming familiar. It is quite difficult to find the texts of many kinds of spell for this very reason. They are jealously guarded by those who know them and are handed down from generation to generation as secrets that, like magical treasure in some stories and myths, will lose their value if exposed to the light of day or to the wrong eyes. This explains in part the rather strange notions most people have of the nature of spells; they have only been allowed to perceive the tip of the iceberg. Nevertheless the assiduous searcher can discover examples of most kinds of spell if he so wishes, and one of the kinds he will find easiest to discover is the incantation, which is the subject of the next chapter.

3

Incantations

I will sow and I will reap
and I will spin your mind asleep

Anon

The word *incantation* is used to describe not only a certain kind
of spell, but also a mode of speech which may be used in the
making and speaking of many different kinds of spell. As·a spell
it is intended, like the invocation, to "inflame with prayer," but it
does not address any one named power. It is also, like the
Invocation, a preparatory spell. It places the spell-maker in a
specific desired state of mind. As a mode of speech it is used in
many kinds of spell, including invocations. It takes the form of a
chant, made up of cumulative repetitions not only of key words and
phrases but also of syntactical and even metrical shapes and
patterns, as well as a definite cadence. Each statement of line is
likely to have the same, or almost the same, cadence as that
preceding or following it, though, of course, in a complex incantation there may be more than one group of similar cadences. The
reason for this is quite simple. The object of incantations is to put
the conscious critical intelligence to sleep so that the intuitive
element can have full play, and so that the "message" may be
transmitted without qualifications by the conscious mind. This is,
in technique, similar to that of hypnosis and the Hindu mantra;

the cadence of each succeeding statement presents no surprises; the tone, whether quiet and lulling or vatic and oratorical, is consistent in its appeal to the subject to be receptive to rhythm and image and overall intent rather than to anything more precise. The object of the incantation is also usually to cover all the qualities which are to be brought into play by means of an item-by-item catalogue. Thus in the great incantation called Saint Patrick's Breastplate we see the attributes of God and the necessities of the speaker, all listed in what appears to be a thorough and highly ordered fashion:

I arise today
Through a mighty strength, the invocation of the Trinity,
Through belief in the threeness,
Through confession of the oneness
Of the Creator of Creation.

I arise today
Through the strength of Christ's birth with His baptism,
Through the strength of His crucifixion with His burial,
Through the strength of His resurrection with His ascension,
Through the strength of His descent for the judgement of Doom.

I arise today
Through the strength of the love of Cherubim,
In obedience of angels,
In the service of archangels,
In hope of resurrection to meet with reward,
In prayers of patriarchs,
In predictions of prophets,
In preachings of apostles,
In faiths of confessors,
In innocence of holy virgins,
In deeds of righteous men.

I arise today
Through the strength of heaven:
Light of sun,
Radiance of moon,
Splendour of fire,
Speed of lightning,
Swiftness of wind,
Depth of sea,
Stability of earth,
Firmness of rock.

I arise to-day
Through God's strength to pilot me;
God's might to guide me
God's wisdom to guide me
God's eye to look before me,
God's ear to hear me,
God's word to speak for me,
God's hand to guard me,
God's way to lie before me,
God's shield to protect me,
God's host to save me
From snares of devils,
From temptation of vices,
From everyone who wishes me ill
Afar and anear
Alone and in a multitude.

I summon today all these powers between me and those evils:
Against every cruel merciless power that may oppose my body
    and soul;
Against incantations of false prophets
Against black laws of Pagandom
Against false laws of heretics,
Against craft of idolatry,
Against spells of women and smiths and wizards,
Against every knowledge that corrupts man's body and soul.

Christ to shield me to-day
Against poison, against burning,
Against drowning, against wounding,
So that there may come to me abundance of reward.
Christ with me, Christ before me, Christ behind me,
Christ in me, Christ beneath me, Christ above me,
Christ on my right hand, Christ on my left,
Christ when I lie down, Christ when I sit down, Christ when I
   arise,
Christ in the heart of every man who thinks of me,
Christ in the mouth of everyone who speaks of me,
Christ in every eye that sees me,
Christ in every ear that hears me.

I arise to-day
Through a mighty strength, the invocation of the Trinity:
Through belief in the Threeness,
Through confession of the Oneness
Of the Creator of Creation.[1]

I have given the whole of this poem, which is also known as *The Deer's Cry*, because it illustrates certain aspects of the incantation so completely. Firstly, the speaker calls on the power of the Trinity, then the power granted man by Christ's life on earth, then the power of the whole church of God, from the highest angelic powers to the "righteous men." He then lists the powers of the natural world, and lists the ways in which God enables him to make use of his own human life. After this he summons up all these powers to stand between him and evil, and enumerates the evils from which he desires to be protected, binding these evils and dominating them by virtue of having already summoned up and invoked the power of God. The incantation ends by listing all the ways in which Christ's presence permeates his days and concludes with a final invocation, a final assertion of the confidence and power which the whole incantation has given him.

The incantation is classic in that it is obviously intended to put the speaker into a desired state of mind rather than to influence or affect phenomena external to him. It is partly a matter of auto-suggestion, perhaps even of self-hypnosis. It does as I earlier described the incantation as doing; it enables "the mind and the psyche to reach a required level of feeling and receptivity." The incantation is often lengthy, because the process of developing, item by item, the catalogue of qualities and establishing power over and through them, while building up to a certainty, naturally takes more time than a spell which has only to send a brief message of a specific kind. Another example of the full-length incantatory spell, which is not a classic of its type in that the end sought is an effect upon phenomena external to the speaker, is the Charm of the Churn (*Eolas a Chrannachain*) from the *Carmina Gadelica*:

Come will the free, come;
Come will the bond, come;
Come will the bells, come;
Come will the maers, come;
Come will the blade, come;
Come will the sharp, come;
Come will the hounds, come;
Come will the wild, come;
Come will the mild, come;
Come will the kind, come;
Come will the loving, come;
Come will the squint, come;
Come will he of the yellow cap,
That will set the churn a-running.

The free will come,
The bond will come,
The bells will come,
The maers will come,
The blades will come,
The sharp will come,
The hounds will come,
The wild will come,
The mild will come,
The kind will come,
The loving will come,

The devious will come,
The brim-full of the glove will come,
To set the churn a-running;
The kindly Columba will come in his array,
And the golden-haired Bride of the kine.

A splash is here,
A plash is here,
A plash is here,
A splash is here,
A crash is here,
A squash is here,
A squash is here,
A crash is here,
A big soft snail is here,
The sap of each of the cows is here,
A thing better than honey and spruce,
A bogle yellow and fresh is here.

A thing better than right is here,
The fist of the big priest is here,
A thing better than the carcase is here,
The head of the dead man is here,
A thing better than wine is here,
The full of the cog of Caristine
Of live thing soft and fair are here,
   Of live things soft and fair are here.

Come, thou churn, come;
Come, thou churn, come;
Come, though life; (?) come, thou breath; (?)
Come, thou churn, come;
Come, thou churn, come;
Come, thou cuckoo; come, thou jackdaw;
Come, thou churn, come;
Come, thou churn, come;
Come will the little lark from the sky,
Come will the little carlin of the black-cap.

Come, thou churn, come;
Come, thou churn, come;
Come will the merle, come will the mavis,
Come will the music from the bower;
Come, thou churn, come;
Come, thou churn, come;
Come, thou wild cat,
To ease thy throat;
Come, thou churn, come;
Come, thou churn, come.

Come, thou hound, and quench thy thirst;
Come, thou churn, come;
Come, thou churn, come;
Come, thou poor; come, thou naked;
Come, thou churn, come;
Come, thou churn, come;
Come, ye alms-deserver
Of most distressful moan;
Come, thou churn, come;
Come, thou churn, come;
Come, each hungry creature,
And satisfy the thirst of thy body.

Come, thou churn, come;
Come, thou churn, come;
It is the God of the elements who bestowed on us,
And not the charm of a carlin with plant.
Come, thou churn, come;
Come, thou churn, come;
Come, thou fair-white Mary,
And endow to me my means;
Come, thou churn, come;
Come, thou churn, come;
Come, thou beauteous Bride,
And bless the substance of my kine.

Come, thou churn, come;
Come, thou churn, come;
The churning made of Mary,
In the fastness of the glen,
To decrease her milk,
To increase her butter;
Butter-milk to wrist,
Butter to elbow;
    Come, thou churn, come;
    Come, thou churn, come.[2]

This, in its resolute cataloguing, reveals another aspect of the spell or charm. It must present a complete list of the attributes it commands to effect the change required; it must miss nothing out or the spell will fail. It should also, if a process of change is required, present the process of change accurately step by step. In this it indicates the belief in sympathetic magic which lies behind many, if not all, spells. If we wish something to happen we can make it happen by presenting a mime of it, a recitation of it, a verbal simulacrum of it. Just as the spitting upon a stone is thought by some to bring rain because the action of the rain falling has been mimed, so the turning of the milk to butter must be mimed detail by detail in the charm for the churn. Another aspect of this particular spell, which applies to a number of "work spells," is that the length of the spell should take roughly the amount of time that the action it describes, and in this case accompanies, should take. Just as sea-shanties are always long enough for the work on the capstan to be completed, so work-spells take the time required to perform the action they accompany and affect.

But not all incantatory spells involve the patterning and cataloguing of the element. Some, indeed, may be constructed almost completely of one repeated statement with just enough variation to ensure that there is a progression from beginning to completion within the spell. This is the case with a Hebridean spell to cure a stye. This incantatory spell is particularly fascinating in that it is accompanied by simple repeated actions which are clearly reinforcements of the spell but not the essential part of the magic, and which obviously have a great deal of suggestive power for the sufferer. It is also interesting in that we see once again the combination of pre-Christian and Christian attitudes in the one charm. The preliminary note to the charm in the *Carmina Gadelica* gives us a dramatic and fascinating account of the whole process:

> The exorcism of the stye is variously called "*Cunntas an t-Sleamhnain*"–Counting of the Stye, "*Eolas an t-Sleamhnain*"–Exorcism of the Stye, and "*Eoir an t-Sleamhnain*"–Charm of the Stye.
>
> When making the charm the exorcist holds some sharp-pointed instrument, preferably a nail or the tongue of a brooch or buckle, between the thumb and forefinger of the right hand. With each question the operator makes a feint with the instrument at the stye, going perilously near the eye. The sensation caused by the thrusting is extremely painful to the sufferer and even to the observer.
>
> The reciter assured the writer that a cure immediately follows the operation. Possibly the thrusting acts upon the nervous system of the patient.
>
> Ordinarily the exorcist omits mentioning the word "*sleamhnan*" after the first two times, abbreviating thus:

> Why came the two here
> Without the three here?

After the incantation the Lord's Prayer is intoned, and the following is repeated:

> Pater one,
> Pater two,
> Pater three,
> Pater four,
> Pater five,
> Pater six,
> Pater seven,
> Pater eight,
> Pater nine,

Pater one
And eight,
Pater of Christ the kindly
Be upon thee to-night,
Pater of the Three of life
Upon thine eye without harm.*

Why came the one stye,
Without the two styes here?
Why came the two styes,
Without the three styes here?
Why came the three styes,
Without the four styes here?
Why came the four styes,
Without the five styes here?
Why came the five styes,
Without the six styes here?
Why came the six styes,
Without the seven styes here?
Why came the seven styes,
Without the eight styes here?
Why came the eight styes,
Without the nine styes here?
why came the nine,
Or one at all here?[3]

This spell is also interesting in that, by means of an incantatory and cumulative series of questions, it does not so much tell the stye to go away as enquire, forcefully, why it is there at all. This spell of the unanswerable question, as we might term it, is definitely one of those messages directed straight at the patient's psyche. The patient's psyche is being told, by implication, that there is no good reason for the stye to be there; therefore the psyche is bound to make the stye disappear. This assumption by the spell that the psyche of the patient will act sensibly and reasonably when reason

* This seems to indicate that the Lord's Prayer was originally repeated nine times.

is given to it is one which lies behind a great deal of healing magic, as we shall see when we devote particular attention to spells of healing.

In the case of the charm to cure a stye, the incantation is intended to hypnotize the subject rather than the speaker, though, of course, the speaker himself must be mastered by the incantation sufficiently to enable him to put out the "power" or "message" of the spell effectively and without self-conscious hesitations or qualifications.

We have now seen three incantations. The first was a classic incantation, the second a work-spell in incantatory form, and the third an incantatory healing spell. In each case the incantation itself formed the whole of the verbal part of the magical act. In the following *Death Rite of the Gabon Pygmies* the incantation is used to create a state of mind which causes the power whose presence is commanded in the closing invocation to be receptive to the command. Once again the incantation patterns fully and precisely the required state of mind, and once again there is a progression in the way the catalogue is presented. This spell is for two voices. The eldest son of the deceased begins the song and the answering refrain is sung by an uncle on the mother's side.

> The animal runs, it passes, it dies. And it is the great cold.
> *It is the great cold of the night, it is the dark.*
> The bird flies, it passes, it dies. And it is the great cold.
> *It is the great cold of the night, it is the dark.*
> The fish flees, it passes, it dies. And it is the great cold.
> *It is the great cold of the night, it is the dark.*
> Man eats and sleeps. He dies. And it is the great cold.
> *It is the great cold of the night, it is the dark.*
> There is light in the sky, the eyes are extinguished, the star
>   shines.
> *The cold is below, the light is on high.*
> The man has passed, the shade has vanished, the prisoner is free!
>   Khvum, Khvum, come in answer to our call![4]

This spell is an excellent example of the incantation that involves several voices. Here there are only two. In other incantations the responses, the answering refrains, may be spoken or sung by a number of people as they are in the case of the responses in many Christian church services. Indeed it is interesting to place an Anglican formula alongside the pygmy one, and note the similarities in structure and in intent. Here is the second half of the Anglican Litany:

We sinners do beseech thee to hear us, O Lord God: and that it may please thee to rule and govern thy holy Church universal in the right way,
We beseech thee to hear us, good Lord.

That it may please thee to keep and strengthen in the true worshipping of thee, in righteousness and holiness of life, thy Servant ELIZABETH, our most gracious Queen and Governor,
We beseech thee to hear us, good Lord.

That it may please thee to rule her heart in thy faith, fear, and love, and that she may evermore have affiance in thee, and ever seek thy honour and glory,
We beseech to hear us, good Lord.

That it may please thee to be her defender and keeper, giving her the victory over all her enemies,
We beseech thee to hear us, good Lord.

That it may please thee to bless and preserve *Elizabeth* the Queen Mother, *Philip* Duke of Edinburgh, *Charles* Prince of Wales, and all the Royal Family,
We beseech thee to hear us, good Lord.

That it may please thee to illuminate all Bishops, Priests, and all Deacons, with true knowledge and understanding of thy Word; and that both by their preaching and living they may set it forth and shew it accordingly.
We beseech thee to hear us, good Lord.

That it may please thee to endue the Lords of the Council, and all the Nobility, with grace, wisdom, and understanding,
We beseech thee to hear us, good Lord.

That it may please thee to bless and keep the Magistrates, giving them grace to execute justice, and to maintain truth,
We beseech thee to hear us, good Lord.

That it may please thee to bless and keep all thy people,

We beseech thee to hear us, good Lord.

That it may please thee to give to all nations unity, peace, and concord,

We beseech thee to hear us, good Lord.

That it may please thee to give us an heart to love and dread thee, and diligently to live after thy commandments,

We beseech thee to hear us, good Lord.

That it may please thee to give to all thy people increase of grace, to hear meekly thy Word, and to receive it with pure affection, and to bring forth the fruits of the Spirit,

We beseech thee to hear us, good Lord.

That it may please thee to bring into the way of truth all such as have erred, and are deceived,

We beseech thee to hear us, good Lord.

That it may please thee to strengthen such as do stand; and to comfort and help the weak-hearted; and to raise up that fall; and finally to beat down Satan under our feet,

We beseech thee to hear us, good Lord.

That it may please thee to succour, help, and comfort all that are in danger, necessity, and tribulation,

We beseech thee to hear us, good Lord.

That it may please thee to preserve all that travel by land or by water, all women labouring of child, all sick persons, and young children; and to shew thy pity upon all prisoners and captives,

We beseech thee to hear us, good Lord.

That it may please thee to defend, and provide for, the fatherless children, and widows, and all that are desolate and oppressed,

We beseech thee to hear us, good Lord.

That it may please thee to forgive our enemies, persecutors, and slanderers, and to turn their hearts,

We beseech thee to hear us, good Lord.

That it may please thee to give us true repentance; to forgive us all our sins, negligences, and ignorances; and to endue us with the grace of thy Holy Spirit, to amend our lives according to thy holy Word,

We beseech thee to hear us, good Lord.
Son of God: we beseech thee to hear us.
Son of God: we beseech thee to hear us.
O Lamb of God: that takest away the sins of the world;
Grant us thy peace.
O Lamb of God: that takest away the sins of the world;
Have mercy upon us.
O Christ, hear us.
O Christ, hear us.
Lord have mercy upon us.
Lord, have mercy upon us.
Christ, have mercy upon us.
Christ, have mercy upon us.
Lord, have mercy upon us.
Lord, have mercy upon us.

Though the incantation here is not preparatory to an invocation but is itself an invocation, the pattern of allusions follows a progressive line of development as in the pygmy spell. As with the Anglican Church so it is with many other churches and religions. The Coppermine Eskimo have a song which is accompanied by a dance whose clear intent is to conjure up the spirit of the great hunter to improve the tribe's hunting skills. The leader of the dance sings the main lines and the remainder of the dancers the refrain:

He constantly bends it, he constantly sends it straight,
The big bow, he constantly sends it straight.

He constantly bends it,
He constantly bends it.

Just as he seeks well for words in a song,
The big bow, he constantly sends it straight.

He constantly bends it,
He constantly bends it.

He constantly bends it as he walks along,
In summer as he walks along.

He constantly bends it,
He constantly bends it.

It is clearly easy to shoot big birds,
As he carries his pack walking along.

He constantly bends it,
He constantly bends it.[5]

This incantation is, in its way, subtle, for while there is a magical intention there is no overt expression of magic, there is no command or appeal in it. It is simply believed that the creation, by song, of the ideal hunter, of the hero, will bring that hero's qualities to the community and thus help it in its hunting activities. The opposite of this kind of incantation is the direct commanding incantation, which may be little more than a listing. Thus in Tuamotua the Creator God, Kio, is supposed to have given his power to Oatea by means of the following incantation, which enumerates all the parts of the speaker's body, and therefore by implication all the attributes of the speaker:

Take hold of my flattened-crown
Take hold of my wrinkled-brow
Take hold of my observing-eye
Take hold of my obstructed-nose
Take hold of my conversing-mouth
Take hold of my chattering-lips
Take hold of my flower-decked-ears
Take hold of my distorted-chin
Take hold of my descending-saliva
Take hold of my crooked-neck
Take hold of my broad-chest
Take hold of my contracted-hands
Take hold of my grasping-fingers
Take hold of my pinching-nails
Take hold of my flexed-side
Take hold of my bulging-ribs
Take hold of my inset-navel
Take hold of my princely-belly

Take hold of my small-of-the-back
Take hold of my swollen-penis
Take hold of my tightly-drawn-testicles
Take hold of my evacuating-rectum
Take hold of my twisted-knee
Take hold of my splay-foot
Take hold of my given-over body[6]

This incantation is clearly the most simple kind we have yet encountered. If not spoken with considerable force and in a "special voice" it would seem to be little but a catalogue, and a rather grotesque catalogue at that. But in the spell-maker's "special voice," it takes on a new power. As I have already said, incantations are invariably designed to be chanted or sung, and nearly all other types of spell benefit from being recited in a voice different from the speaker's ordinary tones. It is almost as if the voice is itself the power. In the Trobriand Islands:

> The mind, *nanola*, by which term intelligence, power of discrimination, capacity for learning magical formulae, and all forms of non-manual skill are described as well as moral qualities, resides somewhere in the larynx.... The force of magic does not reside in the things; it resides within man and can escape only through his voice.[7]

Orpingalik, a Netsilik Eskimo, is quoted as saying:

> Songs are thoughts, sung out with the breath when people are moved by great forces and ordinary speech no longer suffices.[8]

In what way does the language of incantation differ from ordinary language? As we have seen, it involves repetition, parallelism, and the use of a list or lists. The language used is often very unlike that of ordinary verbal communication. Its epithets may be heroic or grotesque. It often combines a language of sublime universality with a language of precisely observed detail. The details are carefully selected to pattern the whole of the matter being dealt with. This is noticeable in the rather crude Tuamotua spell, in the Charm for Milking, and in St. Patrick's Breastplate. It is not only the style which makes the incantation "special speech," but also the choice of details and vocabulary.

The techniques of making an incantation are becoming more obvious. If, for example, we wished to rouse a football team to the peak of their efficiency, we could make an incantation that would be something like a patterned rhetorical version of a coach's pep talk. We would not, of course, say "Go in and kill 'em;" we could, however, list the attributes we wished to intensify. One passage might run:

Let the legs be strong
Let the hands be quick
Let the feet be swift
Let the eyes be keen

We might elaborate this and say:

Let the legs be strong as the redwood trees
Let the hands be quick as the stooping hawk
Let the feet be swift as the racing stream
Let the eyes be keen as the hunting arrow

Or possibly we might use not the commanding incantation but the assertive one and say:

Our limbs are strong with the strength
    of the redwood trees
Our hands are quick as the stoop
    of the hunting hawk

and so forth.

We might, after some thought, pick up a name which would embody for us all the spirit of power. Such a name should perhaps be that of a dead hero or of a god. The living hero may, after all, be concerned with other and material matters. The dead hero is a spirit, and is therefore able to spend his powers for us without being side-tracked by mundane matters. Also, to put the matter in another light, it is the dead hero who is likely to impress our psyches most effectively, for he has become myth to us, has actually become the central power name for a whole range of attributes.

Thus a cricketer might address the spirit of W. G. Grace, just as a Catholic might address a saint or an industrialist (possibly) the spirit of Henry Ford Senior. This may seem facetious, but it is no fantasy. If we walk into boardrooms we see, do we not, the ikons of the founders of the firm? In universities we see the holy pictures of the great Alumni. We have Halls of Fame in which the names and portraits of our heroes are gathered together. Moreover, I defy anyone of any experience in life at all to say that he or she has not at one time or another addressed a supplication, however brief, and however ironic it may have been, to some portrait in the house or at the office. We do, in fact, invoke these powers habitually. Listen to the politicians. Listen to the auctioneer. Listen to the huckster in the street market. And I wonder just how many of us have found ourselves, in a state of induced euphoria, applauding orators, or bidding at auctions for goods we do not really need or even wish to have.

When I say that incantations can be made today, therefore, I am only saying that we can improve upon the quality of the incantations that are already a part of our lives. We can recognize the deep-seated belief in incantatory power which is in each one of us, and we can enhance the quality of our work and our minds by sending these powerful messages to ourselves by means of this technique. We can also use the method of incantation, which is one of the basic methods of spell-makers and one of the least difficult technically, to make spells of blessing and healing which can improve the quality of our lives and help those around us.

Blessings and Protection

4

Blessings and Protection

*Those that guard
and those that bless
share in time
life's timelessness.*

Anon

Incantation is used as a medium of persuasion in many activities of our day-to-day life, as I have already pointed out. Another kind of spell which appears with almost equal frequency is the *blessing*. Like the incantation, and like most kinds of spell, it appears in a somewhat degenerate or truncated form as when we say, in thanks, "Bless you," or "God bless you." In Ireland it is still not uncommon for a man entering a room in which there are a number of people to say "God bless all here," and priests of many religious persuasions still offer blessings to their flock, as does the Pope on Easter Sunday, standing in his balcony overlooking St. Peter's Square and blessing the world. In most of these cases, however, the blessing lacks that particularity which distinguishes the spell proper from the spell gesture. The priest may be sufficiently aware of the meaning and the power of "God" to infuse a quite precise intent into his blessing, but for most of us the intent is simply a generally benevolent one without much force or direction.

If we look at the complete blessing presented to us as parts of religious ritual, or as parts of magical procedures, we notice immediately that the "gifts" are specific. If we read the old folk stories and those legends and myths which have so often come down to us as "fairy stories," again we notice that the blessings are definite and particular. There are stories in which a "fairy godmother," who closely resembles the figure of the white witch, blesses the new-born child with certain qualities of character and physical attributes, and in which the uninvited guest, the black witch, caps the list of blessings with a "gift" which is a curse. The story of the Sleeping Beauty begins with such a christening. In the version given by Ernest Rhys,

> all the fairies began to give their gifts to the princess in the following manner:–
>
> The youngest gave her a gift that she should be the most beautiful person in the world.
>
> The second that she should have wit like an angel.
>
> The third that she should have a wonderful grace in everything that she did.
>
> The fourth that she should sing like a nightingale.
>
> The fifth that she should dance like a flower in the wind.
>
> And the sixth that she would play on all kinds of musical instruments to the utmost degree of perfection.
>
> The old fairy's turn coming next, she advanced forward, and, with a shaking head, that seemed to shew more spite than age, she said,–that the princess, when she was fifteen years old, would have her hand pierced with a spindle, and die of the wound.
>
> This terrible gift made the whole company tremble, and every one of them fell a-crying.
>
> At this very instant the young fairy came out from behind the curtains and spoke these words aloud: "Assure yourselves, O King and Queen, that your daughter shall not die of this disaster. It is true, I have not the power to undo what my elder has done. The princess shall indeed pierce her hand with a spindle; but, instead of dying, she shall only fall into a profound sleep, which shall last a hundred years, at the end of which time a king's son shall come, and awake her from it."[1]

There are other stories in which certain blessings are divided among a group of people. One may be blessed with beauty, one with kindness, one with wisdom, and one with the gift of prophecy. It is not difficult to see how these gifts are made with an air of authority, almost as if they were physical objects which could be handed over as one hands over birthday presents. Not infrequently a blessing makes use of the words "give" or "bring" or "send." It is usually addressed directly to the person or object or a representation of him or it. The blessing does not seek, like the healing spell or the bidding spell, to cure or control. It simply "gives" qualities and attributes.

If we examine various blessing spells we soon discover that there are several different kinds. The first and most easily identifiable kind is the general blessing made in the "name" or "names" of power. Thus we have such blessings as this, from the Hebrides:

My own blessing be with you
The blessing of God be with you
The blessing of Spirit be with you
    and with your children,
    With you and with your children.[2]

And this similarly general blessing from the same place:

The compassing of God be on thee,
    The compassing of the God of life.

The compassing of Christ be on thee,
    The compassing of the Christ of love.

The compassing of Spirit be on thee,
    The compassing of the Spirit of Grace.

The compassing of the Three be on thee,
    The compassing of the Three preserve thee,
    The compassing of the Three preserve thee.[3]

The appeal to "the Three" is here presented in Christian terms. Another Gaelic spell appears to be less attached to Christian belief, and while it does not contain the actual blessing command it is in fact a blessing, and specifically also a spell of protection:

67

The Three Who are over me,
The Three Who are below me,
The Three Who are above me here,
The Three Who are above me yonder;
The Three Who are in the earth,
The Three Who are in the air,
The Three Who are in the heaven,
        The Three Who are in the great pouring sea.[4]

These blessings are all both invocatory and incantatory, and are all-encompassing in intent. The third of them is also a spell of self-blessing and self-protection. There are many kinds of spell in which the speaker or maker seeks either to protect himself or to increase his powers in some fashion. Few of these however, are blessings proper. The great majority of protection spells are directed *against* harm, or even against specific enemies and ills, and many are extremely aggressive. The self-blessing spells are frequently invocations of the kind described earlier, and contain negative elements. These negative elements often derive from the intent to make the blessing exclusive, as in the interesting auto-suggestive spell given by Abragail and Valaria in their entertaining book *How to become a Sensuous Witch*. The spell is preceded by a fairly simple ritual, which is worth some attention because of its implications:

On a night of Venus (Friday) take a bath in lovage root. After drying off, cover your body with oil of musk. Light a red candle and burn a pleasant smelling incense. Stand naked in front of the mirror and, placing your hands on your body, gaze into your eyes (through the mirror) and repeat the following incantations:

Soft my skin as Diana's
Smouldering eyes as Aradia
Sensuous as the goddess, my mother
Fascination for me and no other.

Repeat this three times, feeling the true sensuality of your whole being.[5]

This magic, like a good deal of that presented by followers of witchcraft, combines speech and ritual. The ritual is calculated to create a conviction in the spell-maker that her skin is already soft, that her eyes are already smouldering, and that her body is already sensuous. Thus the ritual provides the emotional certainty necessary to the effective speaking of the spell.

It is important to realize that, in blessings as in other spells, the ritual element which accompanies or precedes the words is very often a means of ensuring the necessary confidence, and of delimiting and defining the intent of the spell-maker rather than being magical in itself.

The self-interested blessing, the self-indulging spell, is obviously less risky than the curse. Those who have made such spells, however, report that something frequently goes wrong with them. The consequences can be amusing—if one is able to laugh at one's own discomfiture. One spell-maker I know possesses a figure which has the attribute of granting wealth. One day, in some financial difficulty, but not in enough trouble for the spell to be a necessity, she asked for money. Money she found, to the tune of fifteen cents. Another case I know is of a man who asked the Goddess for money. He used formal and poetic language in his spell, and asked for "rivers of gold" and "showers of silver." Within an hour of making his spell, he received a parcel from friends in Greece. The parcel contained two small phials of water from the springs of Helicon sacred to the Muse; one of the bottles had a golden label and the other a silver one.

The second story has two morals. The first is that it is folly to ask for money. The second is that the Power is capable of what seems uncommonly like deliberate misunderstanding. This last point is important. If you wish to bless a person you love with great happiness, you may find that the success of your spell results in a relationship which excludes you. If you bless a person with peace of mind you may find that everything you liked about that person has altered.

Such "misunderstandings" occur particularly frequently with spells of self-interest, for, while it is relatively easy to be precise as to one's desires for someone else, one's desires for oneself are frequently complex. Moreover even the wisest among us mistake our needs. One kind of self-blessing spell, however, is difficult to make mistakes with. This is the spell which asks for increased perception, for vision, rather than specific blessings. There is no way in which such a message can be misunderstood by the deep mind or interpreted as being a piece of self indulgence. To ask for increased awareness is always good. An interesting example of spells for vision is that recorded in F. Bruce Lamb's *Wizard of the Upper Amazon*. While the spells are made as an accompaniment, initially, to the creation of a hallucinogen from the "vision vine," the *Nixi Honi*, and later precede the drinking of the liquid, it is clear that the spells are themselves essential to the whole process. Indeed the magician is directing the drug to have certain positive effects, to be beneficial. In the language of the middle of the twentieth century, he is ensuring a "good trip," just as the Hebridean plant-gatherer ensured successful healing by addressing the healing herbs he plucked. In the final instance, of course, the adept and disciplined spell-maker may be able to do without the drug altogether. The preparation of the liquid, the *honi xuma*, is described thus:

First the vine was cut into one-foot pieces with the stone ax and pounded on a flat stone with a large wooden mallet until it was well mashed.
The old man chanted:

Nixi honi, vision vine
boding spirit of the forest
origin of our understanding
give up your magic power
to our potion
illuminate our mind
bring us foresight
show us the designs
of our enemies
expand our understanding
of our forest

A layer of mashed vine pieces was then carefully arranged in the bottom of a large new clay pot. On top of this was laid a layer of the leaves in the shape of a fan. And as he did this Nixi chanted:

> Bush with markings of the serpent
> give us your leaves
> for our potion
> bring us favor
> of the boa
> source of good fortune

Then alternating layers of mashed vine and leaves were put in place until the pot was more than half full. Clear water from the stream was then added until the plant material was well covered.

A slow fire was started under the pot and the cooking was maintained at a very low simmer for many hours until the liquid was reduced to less than half.

When the cooking process was completed the fire was removed and, after cooling, the plant material was withdrawn from the liquid. After several hours of further cooling and settling, the clear green liquid was carefully dipped off into small clay pots, each fitted with a tight cover.

The entire process took three days, being done with utter calmness and deliberation. The interminable chants accompanied each step, invoking the spirits of the vine, the shrub and the other forest spirits.[6]

The actual use of the liquid was preceded by other spells. The magician and his companion went together into the forest.

He led the way toward the forest at his usual slow, deliberate walk, which also gave the impression of great age. He seemed to choose each step with care. On the way he started a low chant, seemingly to himself:

> Spirits of the forest
> revealed to us by *honi xuma*
> bring us knowledge of the realm
> assist in the guidance of our people
> give us the stealth of the boa

penetrating sight of the hawk and the owl
acute hearing of the deer
brute endurance of the tapir
grace and strength of the jaguar
knowledge and tranquillity of the moon
kindred spirits, guide our way

It was a clear, still day of the early dry season. A few isolated cotton puffs of clouds drifted in an azure sky as we stepped from the village clearing into the mottled shade of the cool forest. Preparations had been made for our arrival, but no one was present. The old man sounded a birdcall that was answered from somewhere out of sight.

I looked around. A tiny, newly kindled fire glowed in the center of a small opening in the forest undergrowth. Beside it was a bunch of the leaves used for the fragrant ceremonial smoke. The small clearing revealed the massive buttresses to the columns that supported the leafy roof of the forest a hundred feet above our heads. These columns, draped in vines and hanging plants, were also visible in the diffuse filtered light that was occasionally broken by a brilliant shaft of direct sunlight. Details otherwise unnoticed would stand out momentarily in vivid clarity in these illuminating shafts of light from above.

At a motion from the chief, I sat down comfortably in a hammock swung low outside the shelter. Chanting, the old man deliberately put a bunch of leaves on the fire. Billowing clouds of fragrant smoke filled the still air.

O most powerful spirit
of the bush with the fragrant leaves
we are here again to seek wisdom
give us tranquillity and guidance
to understand the mysteries of the forest
the knowledge of our ancestors

We savored the fragrant tranquillity of the scene as the smoke drifted around us and up into the vaulted structure of the forest. Every immediate sound and movement seemed suspended by the magic smoke. Before the enchanted spell drifted away with the smoke, Xumu poured a single large gourd cupful of *honi xuma* from a pot and began another low chant:

Phantom revealing spirit of the vine
we seek your guidance now
to translate the past into the future
to understand every detail of our milieu
to improve our life
reveal the secrets that we need

He came over to me and said: "You drink alone this time. I will be present to guide you. All is well. Your preparations have been completed. Every reaction is favorable. Drink it all at once, without hurry and without fear, and prepare for visions. Pleasant and profound visions will come to you."[7]

Many self-blessing spells are attached to the picking of a particular herb of protection, as is the case with the Gaelic spell to be made at the gathering of St. Columba's Plant, otherwise also known as St. John's Wort:

Plantlet of Columba,
Without seeking, without searching,
Plantlet of Columba,
Under my arm for ever!
For luck of men,
For luck of means,
For luck of wish (?),
For luck of sheep,
For luck of goats,
For luck of birds,
For luck of fields,
For luck of shell-fish,
For luck of fish,
For luck of produce and kine,
For luck of progeny and people,
For luck of battle and victory,
On land, on sea, on ocean,

Through the Three on high,
Through the Three a-nigh,
Through the Tree eternal,
Plantlet of Columba,
I cull thee now,
    I cull thee now.[8]

Spells must be precise as well as whole-hearted. Indeed, many blessing spells are as carefully detailed in their structure and in their commands as are the invocations and incantations we have already examined. Here is a beautifully patterned Hebridean blessing:

Wisdom of serpent be thine,
Wisdom of raven be thine,
    Wisdom of valiant eagle.

Voice of swan be thine,
Voice of honey be thine,
    Voice of the son of the stars.

Bounty of sea be thine,
Bounty of land be thine,
    Bounty of the Father of heaven.[9]

Here is a less general blessing, also from the Hebrides, which is in the form of a prayer:

Bless, O God, my little cow,
    Bless, O God, my desire;
Bless Thou my partnership
    And the milking of my hand, O God.

Bless, O God, each teat,
    Bless, O God, each finger;
Bless Thou each drop
    That goes into my pitcher, O God![10]

The way in which the second stanza of this spell describes the exact sequence of the milking operation emphasizes the necessity of leaving nothing at all significant out of the spell. It also leads us to consider the second point that Huson makes which is central to the spell-maker's discipline. If, as Paracelsus said, every doubt mars the perfection, it is important that in making a spell there should be no hesitations and qualifications, no drawing back. Moreover, spells should not dwell upon the negative aspect of that which they are attempting to offer. It would be a bad spell that, in blessing a man with the gift of peace of mind, dwelt more upon the anxieties and sufferings that the spell was intended to counter than upon the positive blessing itself. Such an emphasis may even reinforce rather than alleviate the ill. This is especially important in healing spells. The spell-maker must envision health, envision the completed blessing, with all his heart. However troubled he may be by the sad state of things, he must not allow thought of it to enter his head while he is making the spell. The same applies to all blessings which are specific in intent and which, either by invocation or by the sympathetic patterning of the desired event or state, intend a general good. Consider, for example, the following Dama spell which calls for rain and for fertility, but which does not mention drought or hunger:

> Father, bless us still!
>   Father, reward us still!
> May the land have onions!
> May it have *ou*-berries!
> May it have ground-nuts!
> May the clouds still rain![11]

This is a prayer for blessing, perhaps, rather than a proper blessing spell, but the distinction between prayers and blessings is difficult to make when the pattern is that of invocation followed by sympathetic patterning of the desired events. A longer blessing from the Osage tribe of North American Indians shows the patterning method clearly. Each line is actually the first line of a stanza, the rest of which is made up of four lines of repetition.

> I have made a footprint, a sacred one.
> I have made a footprint, through it the blades push upward.
> I have made a footprint, through it the blades radiate.

75

I have made a footprint, over it the blades float in the wind.
I have made a footprint, over it the ears lean toward one another.
I have made a footprint, over it I bend the stalk to pluck the
  ears.
I have made a footprint, over it the blossoms lie gray.
I have made a footprint, smoke arises from my house.
I have made a footprint, there is cheer in my house.
I have made a footprint, I live in the light of day.[12]

An interesting exception to the general rule that the spell must avoid reinforcing ills by emphasizing their existence is the Trobriand Islander's spell against hunger. Here, however, one notes that the detailed description of hunger and its pains gives us the sense that, because we have patterned it in words, we are able to control it. Moreover, each description is countered by the repeated word "restore" and the whole spell ends with a powerful assertiveness.

I

Restore, restore . . .
Restore this way, restore that way.
Trumpet shell, restore, restore.

2

Trumpet shell, restore, restore
The hunger-swollen belly, trumpet shell, restore, restore.
The hunger exhaustion, trumpet shell, restore, restore.
The hunger faintness, trumpet shell, restore, restore.
The hunger prostration, trumpet shell, restore, restore.
The hunger depression, trumpet shell, restore, restore.
The hunger drooping, trumpet shell, restore, restore.
The throbbing famine, trumpet shell, restore, restore
The drooping famine, trumpet shell, restore, restore.
Round the *tatum* (house), trumpet shell, restore, restore.
Round the *Kaykatiga* (house) trumpet shell, restore, restore.
Round the earth oven, trumpet shell, restore, restore.
Round the hearth-stones, trumpet shell, restore, restore.
Round the foundation-beams, trumpet shell, restore, restore.

Round the rafters, trumpet shell, restore, restore.
Round the ridge pole, trumpet shell, restore, restore.
Round the front frame of my thatch, trumpet shell, restore,
    restore.
Round the shelves of my house, trumpet shell, restore, restore.
Round the threshold boards of my house, trumpet shell, restore,
    restore.
Round the ground fronting my house, trumpet shell, restore,
    restore.
Round the central place, trumpet shell, restore, restore.
Round the beaten soil, trumpet shell, restore, restore.
Round the *yagesi*, trumpet shell, restore, restore.
Round where the road starts, trumpet shell, restore, restore.
Round the roads themselves, trumpet shell, restore, restore.
Round the seashore, trumpet shell, restore, restore.
Round the low-water mark, trumpet shell, restore, restore.
Round the shallow water, trumpet shell, restore, restore.
Restore this way, restore that way.

3
This is not thy wind, O hunger, thy wind is from the north-
    west.
This is not thy sea-passage, the sea-passage of Kadinaka is thy
    sea-passage.
This is not thy mountain, the hill in Wawela is thy mountain.
This is not thy promontory, the promontory of Silawotu is thy
    promontory.
This is not thy channel, the channel in Kalubaku is thy channel.
This is not thy sea-arm, the passage of Kaulokoki is thy
    sea-arm.
Get thee to the passage between Tuma and Buriwada.
Get thee to Tuma.
Disperse, begone.
Get old, begone.
Die away, begone.
Die for good and all, begone.

I sweep thee, O belly of my village.
The belly of my village boils up.
The belly of my village is darkened with plenty
The belly of my village is full of strong beams
The belly of my village streams with sweat
The belly of my village is drenched with sweat.[13]

This is a complex spell because, while its intent is a blessing, it includes a bidding spell in that Hunger is commanded to go elsewhere. Thus, although this is a blessing, it is also a bidding and a binding spell. The binding spell may be a part of a blessing, and usually takes the form of so describing the force that is to be bound that the words themselves appear to have mastered it; once mastered, the bound force can be commanded to leave, or to die, or to do whatever the spell-maker intends. The blessing part of the spell is then possible, and the patterned and sympathetic description of good can be given and known to be effective. This is, in many ways, the verbal equivalent of the long-practised magical ritual of creating the wax model of the person you wish to affect and then operating upon it. It is a use, within the purely verbal spell, of sympathetic magic.

The binding element is of course quite inseparable from the sympathetic element, for the patterning of an event, the naming of the names, is itself an act of binding, a controlling. The blessing may even consist almost entirely of the naming and binding, as in the eskimo spell for rain which runs:

Clouds, clouds,
Clouds, clouds down below,
Clouds, clouds,
Clouds, clouds down below.[14]

Some blessings are, of course, directed not at the natural elements, nor at people, but at objects. In many societies agricultural implements are blessed, either upon their creation or before their being used. Ships are blessed at their naming with the words, "I name this ship ———; may God bless all who sail in her." This kind of blessing differs little from acts of consecration and dedication

which form a part of many religio-magical rituals. According to
Paul Huson, the Witch's cord is blessed with the words

Made to measure,
wrought to bind,
blessed be
thou cord entwined.[15]

Here the function (in this instance magical) of the object is
described and then blessed. It is the same with blessings upon all
implements. The effectiveness of this kind of spell might be
doubted. A well-blessed plough may, after all, be handled badly by
an inept ploughman. Nevertheless it is well known that in the use
of any implement the confidence of the user plays a great part in
contributing to the implement's efficiency. And conversely, it is
clear that doubts as to the efficiency of one's tools make for poor
workmanship. To what extent the blessed, or cursed, implement is
effective or ineffective if its user is not aware that it has either been
blessed or cursed it is hard to determine. Nevertheless there are
good reasons to believe that psychic energy of the kind we have been
discussing can be retained, and even emitted, by objects which have
been subjected to "radiations" from the "deep mind" of some
human being, whether these radiations were voluntary or involun-
tary. All rites of purification and exorcism, as well as all forms of
divination by means of personal possessions and much sympathetic
magic, stem from this belief. So the blessing of an implement may
be more than a way to make its user confident; it may be the actual
implantation of important and helpful messages which the user
will, if at all receptive to such messages, receive and obey.

The most significant and widespread form of blessing objects, as
distinct from people, is the blessing on the dwelling place. This has
been a part of most societies for thousands of years. Here is a full-
scale *Blessing of a House* from the *Carmina Gadelica*:

May God give blessing
    To the house that is here;

May Jesus give blessing
    To the house that is here;

May Spirit give blessing
  To the house that is here;

May Three give blessing
  To the house that is here;

May Brigit give blessing
  To the house that is here;

May Michael give blessing
  To the house that is here;

May Mary give blessing
  To the house that is here;

May Columba give blessing
  To the house that is here;

Both crest and frame,
  Both stone and beam;

Both clay and wattle,
  Both summit and foundation;

Both window and timber,
  Both foot and head;

Both man and woman,
  Both wife and children;

Both young and old,
  Both maiden and youth (?);

Plenty of food,
Plenty of drink,
Plenty of beds,
  Plenty of ale;

Much of riches,
Much of mirth,
Many of people,
Much of long life
  Be ever there:

Both warrior and poet,
  Both clay and beam;

Both gear and thong,
  Both crook and tie;

Both bairn and begetter,
  Both wife and children;

Both young and mature,
  Both maiden and youth (?);

May the King of the elements
  Be its help,
  The king of glory
    Have charge of it;

Christ the beloved,
  Son of Mary Virgin,
  And the gentle Spirit
    Be pouring therein;

Michael, bright warrior,
  King of the angels,
  Watch and ward it
    With the power of his sword;

And Brigit, the fair and tender,
  Her hue like the cotton-grass,
  Rich-tressed maiden
    Of ringlets of gold;

Mary, the fair and tender,
  Be nigh the hearth,
  And Columba kindly
  Giving benediction
  In fulfilment of each promise
    On those within,
    On those within![16]

This is a most positive spell, but it implies a feeling that the blessing is a necessary protective device. This also applies to the blessing spell that is still most commonly used in our culture, the lullaby. Some lullabies are simply reassuring, as is the simple:

Hush-a-bye baby,
    Daddy is near,
Mammy's a lady,
    And that's very clear.[17]

Others are obviously partially or wholly spells, as:

Sleep, baby, sleep,
Thy father guards the sheep;
Thy mother shakes the dreamland tree
And from it fall sweet dreams for thee,
    Sleep, baby, sleep.

Sleep, baby, sleep,
Our cottage vale is deep;
The little lamb is on the green,
With woolly fleece so soft and clean—
    Sleep, baby, sleep.

Sleep, baby, sleep,
Down where the woodbines creep;
Be always like the lamb so mild,
A kind and sweet and gentle child,
    Sleep, baby, sleep.[18]

Here the imagery is reassuring also, but the lullaby commands the child to do more than sleep. It seeks also to make him a gift of the mildness of the lamb. Another verse sometimes used by a child at bedtime is well known and has many variants. The version given by Aubrey in the seventeenth century runs:

Matthew, Mark, Luke, John
Bless the bed that I lye on;
And blessed guardian angel keep
Me safe from danger while I sleep[19]

This can be changed into the second person singular and used as a spell of blessing rather than as a self-protective spell. Some lullabies make great use of the notion of guardian spirits, like this German evensong:

Fourteen angels in a band
Every night around me stand.
Two to my left hand,
Two to my right,
Who watch me ever
By day and night.
Two at my head
Two at my feet,
To guard my slumber
Soft and sweet;
Two to wake me
At break of day,
When night and darkness
Pass away;
Two to cover me
Warm and nice,
And two to lead me
To Paradise.[20]

This is simple and direct. Some of the Italian lullabies are more complicated and involve spell-making more obviously, as in:

O Sleep, O Sleep, O thou beguiler, Sleep,
Beguile this child, and in beguilement keep,
Keep him three hours, and keep him moments three;
Until I call beguile this child for me.
And when I call I'll call:—My root, my heart,
The people say my only wealth thou art.
Thou art my only wealth; I tell thee so.
Now, bit by bit, this boy to sleep will go;
He falls and falls to sleeping bit by bit,
Like the green wood what time the fire is lit,
Like to green wood that never flame can dart,
Heart of thy mother, of the father heart!

Like to green wood, that never flame can shoot.
Sleep thou, my cradled hope, sleep thou, my root,
My cradled hope, my spirit's strength and stay;
Mother, who bore thee, wears her life away;
Her life she wears away, and all day long
She goes a-singing to her child this song.[21]

A Corsican *ninna-nanna* is even more elaborate, beginning with an idealized and comforting description of the child's life and ending with a powerful blessing:

Hushaby, my darling boy;
Hushaby, my hope and joy.
You're my little ship so brave
Sailing boldly o'er the wave;
One that tempests doth not fear,
Nor the winds that blow from high.
Sleep awhile, my baby dear;
Sleep, my child, and hushaby.

Gold and pearls my vessel lade,
Silk and cloth the cargo be,
All the sails are of brocade
Coming from beyond the sea;
And the helm of finest gold,
Made a wonder to behold.
Fast awhile in slumber lie;
Sleep, my child, and hushaby.

After you were born full soon
You were christened all aright;
Godmother she was the moon,
Godfather the sun so bright;
All the stars in heaven told
Wore their necklaces of gold.
Fast awhile in slumber lie;
Sleep, my child, and hushaby.

Pure and balmy was the air,
Lustrous all the heavens were;
And the seven planets shed
All their virtues on your head;
And the shepherds made a feast
Lasting for a week at least.
Fast awhile in slumber lie;
Sleep, my child, and hushaby.

Nought was heard but minstrelsy,
Nought but dancing met the eye,
In Cassoni's vale and wood
And in all the neighbourhood;
Hawk and Blacklip, stanch and true,
Feasted in their fashion too.
Fast awhile in slumber lie;
Sleep, my child, and hushaby.

Older years when you attain,
You will roam o'er field and plain;
Meadows will with flowers be gay,
And with oil the fountains play,
And the salt and bitter sea
Into balsam changed be.
Fast awhile in slumber lie;
Sleep, my child, and hushaby.

And these mountains, wild and steep,
Will be crowded o'er with sheep,
And the wild goat and the deer
Will be tame and void of fear;
Vulture, fox, and beast of prey,
From these bounds shall flee away.
Fast awhile in slumber lie;
Sleep, my child, and hushaby.

You are savoury, sweetly blowing,
You are thyme, of incense smelling,
Upon Mount Basella growing,
Upon Mount Cassoni dwelling;
You the hyacinth of the rocks
Which is pasture for the flocks.
Fast awhile in slumber lie;
Sleep, my child, and hushaby.[22]

Some protective spells are banning and banishing spells; they
banish the presence of evil or mischief, as in the British:

Saint Francis and Saint Benedict,
Bless this house from wicked wight;
From the Night-mare and the goblin
That is hight Good-Fellow Robin;
Keep it from all evil spirits,
Fairies, weasels, rats and ferrets,
    From curfew-time
    To the next prime.[23]

While this particular spell is taken, not from oral tradition, but
from W. Cartwright's play, *The Ordinary*, it seems likely that it is
based upon current folk-lore and current protection spells.

Some spells are made to protect against specific evils and many
of these combine blessing and cursing elements, as does the Anglo-
Saxon spell against theft:

May nothing I own be stolen or concealed,
any more than Herod could (steal or conceal) our Lord.
I thought of St. Helena,
and I thought of Christ hung on the cross.
So I think I shall find these cattle and they shall not go away far,
and I shall know where they are, and they shall not get lost,
and I shall love them, and they shall not be led away.
Garmund, servant of God,
Find those cattle and bring back those cattle,

have those cattle and keep those cattle,
and bring home those cattle,
that he never has a piece of land to lead them to,
nor a district to carry them to,
nor buildings to confine them in.
If anybody should do so, may it never come off successfully for him.
Within three days I shall know his might,
his force and his protecting powers.
May he quite perish, as wood is consumed by fire,
may he be as fragile as a thistle,
he who plans to drive away these cattle,
or to carry off these goods.   Amen.[24]

A less revengeful spell against theft, also from the Anglo-Saxon, includes a simple ritual which ensures that whatever the path the thief has taken, he will be discovered.

As soon as somebody tells you that your goods are lost, then you must say first of all, before you say anything else:

Bethlehem is the name of the town where Christ was born.
It is well known throughout the whole world.
So may this deed be known among men,
Through the holy cross of Christ.   Amen.

Then worship three times towards the east and say three times:
    The cross of Christ will bring it back from the east.
Then worship three times towards the west and say three times:
    The cross of Christ will bring it back from the west.
Then worship three times towards the south and say three times:
    The cross of Christ will bring it back from the south.
Then worship three times towards the north and say three times:
    The cross of Christ will bring it back from the north.
    The cross of Christ was hidden and it is found.
    The Jews hanged Christ, they treated Him in a most evil way.
    They concealed what they could not keep hidden.
    So may this deed be concealed in no way,
    Through the holy cross of Christ.   Amen.[25]

A self-blessing spell with an interesting combination of ritual magic and Christian elements is the Anglo-Saxon *Journey Charm*:

> I draw a protecting circle round myself with this rod and
>   commend myself to God's grace,
> against the sore stitch, against the sore bite,
> against the fierce horror,
> against the mighty dread that is hateful to everybody,
> and against every evil that invades the land.
> A victory charm I sing, a victory rod I carry,
> victorious in word, victorious in deed, may this avail me.
> May no nightmare disturb me, no powerful enemy oppress me,
> may nothing dreadful ever befall my life.
> But may the Almighty, the Son and the Holy Ghost,
> the Lord worthy of all honour,
> as I have heard, the Creator of heaven, save me.
> Abraham and Isaac and such men,
> Moses and Jacob and David and Joseph,
> and Eve and Anne and Elizabeth,
> Zacharias and also Mary, the mother of Christ,
> and also the brothers Peter and Paul,
> and also a thousand of the angels,
> I call to my help against all foes.
> They conduct and protect me and save my life,
> they keep me and govern me,
> guiding my actions. A hope of glory,
> a hand over my head, (i.e., in blessing) be to me the host of the
>   holy ones,
> the band of victorious saints, the righteous angels.
> I pray to all with glad mind
> that for a blessing and protection,
> Matthew be my helmet, Mark my coat of mail,
> the strong light of my life, Luke my sword,
> sharp and bright-edged, John my shield,
> gloriously adorned, the Seraph of the roads.
> I travel along, I meet friends,

all the glory of angels, the instruction of the blessed one.
I pray for good favour from the God of victory,
for a good voyage, a calm and light
wind to the shores. I have heard of winds,
boiling waters. Ever secure
against all foes, I meet with friends,
that I may live in the peace of the Almighty,
protected from the evil one who seeks my life,
established in the glory of the angels,
and in the holy land, the glory of the kingdom of heaven,
as long as I may live in this life.   Amen.[26]

This is an invocatory spell and involves no cursing or banning, unlike many protective spells, which do their task by "banishing" an evil wisher. These spells are frequently conditional. They start off by saying "If this person has harmed me, then let thus and thus befall him." In this way injustice is avoided. The banning spell can sometimes become quite ferocious, especially when it is intended as a protection against "the evil eye," or, as we would say, the malice of ill-wishers. A powerful example is this:

Whoso laid on thee the eye,
May it lie upon himself,
May it lie upon his house,
May it lie upon his flocks,
On the shuffling carlin,
On the sour-faced carlin,
On the bounding carlin,
On the sharp-shanked carlin,
Who arose in the morning,
With her eye on her flocks,
With her flocks in her "seoin,"
May he never own a fold,
May she never have half her desires,
The part of her which the ravens do not eat,
May the birds devour.

Four made to thee the eye,
Man and dame, youth and maid;
Three who will cast off thee the envy
The Father, the Son, and the Holy Spirit.

As Christ lifted the fruit,
From the branches of the bushes,
May He now lift off thee
Every ailment, every envy, every jealousy,
From this day forth till the last day of thy life.[27]

Here is another, based loosely upon an Assyrian formula.

You, my enemy,
whose words bewitch me,
whose tongue attacks me,
whose lips curse me,
I bind your mouth,
I bind your tongue,
I bind your eyes,
I bind your feet,
I bind your knees,
I bind your hands;
may the evil that you work
destroy your body.[28]

Many spells against evil are accompanied by rituals which pattern in physical images the process which is desired. Consider this charm to avert evil from the Atharva-Veda, which may have been completed as early as 600 B.C. but which certainly does not date from later than A.D. 500.

1. Let me go, O evil; being powerful, take thou pity on us! Set me, O evil, unharmed, into the world of happiness.

2. If, O evil, thou dost not abandon us, then do we abandon thee at the fork of the road. May evil follow after another (man)!

3. Away from us may thousand-eyed, immortal (evil) dwell! Him whom we hate may it strike, and him whom we hate do thou surely smite.[29]

This is recited at night as parched grains of corn are put into a sieve and then thrown away. The following day the spell-maker scatters three handfuls of food on running water as an offering to Sahasraksha, the thousand-eyed one, and throws three balls of rice down at a cross roads where, as the spell commands, the evil will be transferred to another person who happens there.

The notion that an existing evil or sickness cannot simply be cancelled out or healed but must be passed on to someone else or to something else is a very old one. Many such "transference" spells exist, and we find one example in the story of the Gadarene Swine in the Bible. The transference of the "evil" to an object which is then burned or buried or drowned carries conviction to the deep mind, for we have all in early childhood accepted the notion that some things are "bad," "poisonous" or "nasty," and have seen these qualities of "evil" as belonging to something essentially animate and therefore destructible or, at least, cageable. Whether or not "evil" can be actually thus transferred is of no real consequence, for if the deep mind believes it has been transferred, then, to all intents and purposes, that transference has occurred. Similarly, in transferring "evil" from one person into another or into an animal, if the deep mind sends this message of transference with sufficient power it will affect the deep mind of the creature which receives the message, just as a message of healing and blessing will affect its recipient.

This is not to say that it is necessary to think in terms of transferring evil or sickness. Both can be countered by other means, the sickness by healing spells, and the evil by blessings—by those self-blessings which, like the spells of the Wizard of the Upper Amazon, call up good to such an extent as to dwarf, dominate, control, and finally absorb the evil. Moreover, as I have said before, to curse (and the transference spell is, in its way, inevitably a curse) is always to curse the curse-maker; to wish evil upon anyone or anything is to wish evil upon oneself. It is far better to follow the example of St. Patrick and invoke the powers of good for healing, protection, and the furtherance of one's proper life's work.

5

Binding and Bidding

I will bid and I will bind
And I will hold you to my mind

Old Rhyme

The element of binding forms a part of many kinds of spell. We have already seen how, in the Trobriand Islanders' spell against hunger, the spirit of Hunger is first described, and therefore bound, and then commanded to depart. The act of binding is, in many instances, simply an act of description; that which is to be bound, to be controlled, is described in precise detail and usually in a highly patterned form. This is because in our deep mind we believe that once we have patterned something, we can control it; once we have described our longings or our griefs we feel, if only momentarily, that we have mastered them. We have, indeed, usually done so, though to what extent we cannot always tell. It is worth pointing out that a great part of psychiatric practice depends upon the belief that once a person has patterned out, in words or symbols, a problem that is troubling him or a relationship with which he cannot come to terms, the process of mastery and control has begun. We have already referred to this patterning or binding in terms of sympathetic magic. The spell-maker who performs the dance of the coming of the rain is not merely commanding the rain to come but binding the rain-bringing powers by presenting them with a simulacrum of themselves.

Binding spells are not, of course, always the easiest spells to

93

make, for the very term suggests that messages and commands sent out from one's own deep mind may well meet with resistance. One may find in performing a binding spell to control another person's actions that there is so little sympathy for that kind of action within the person concerned that the spell may fail. On the other hand a command that binds a person and seeks to bid them to perform actions towards which they are sympathetic, but for which they have repressed their desires, is frequently astonishingly successful. I am speaking here of binding as if it invariably also includes bidding, or the commanding of certain actions. This is usually the case, although some spell-makers have been known to bind for the sake of binding, to attempt to wholly possess a person's will. This is strong magic indeed, and, like all strong magic connected with the lust for power, accelerates the destructive process within the magician himself.

There are numerous binding techniques, and almost all of them are classed as sympathetic magic by the majority of writers. In order to bind a person, we are often told, we need a portrait of him, and/or a nail paring, a lock of hair, a piece of clothing, or a prized possession. These objects are then laid out in front of the spell-maker as the spell is made. Such objects are simply a means of focusing the spell-maker's attention, of directing his message precisely, and of helping him towards the belief (which is essential) that there is in some way a direct "hot line" from him to the person he wishes to affect. Photographs are most usually used in these days; they are easy to come by, and a group of different photographs can give a good sense of the "all-round" presence of the person.

The objects, laid out in a pattern which seems appropriate to the spell-maker, assist the directing of the spell. The pattern made should not, however, be an enclosed form, especially not a circle, and not a square or triangle, for the deep mind accepts such patterns as excluding energies rather than being vulnerable to them.

But the use of objects is not essential. If the spell-maker is able to visualize the person he wishes to bind with reasonable accuracy and precision, and especially if the person is well known to him, photographs and other objects may not only be unnecessary but, because they present a more approximate picture than that he can provide with his own memory, they may actually become hindrances. In this, as in all other matters of spell-making, however, the spell-maker himself must be the judge of what will be most effective and must operate in accordance with those intuitions provided him by messages from his own deep mind.

In these cases the spell-maker may find it unnecessary to even name the person he is seeking to bind. The spell may begin either after an invocation or without one, with such words as:

Let this person change his mind
Fill it with the ease and calm
Of summer warmth and summer peace
Let him feel within his palm
the tender clasp of hope and love
And ease his brow of every strain
And bless him with a distant home
Where he may learn his truths again[1]

Such a spell is clearly directed towards altering a person's character and making him less anxious, less bitter, than he may be assumed to be; it is also a spell to send him away from the spell-maker. This is a very simple bidding spell, and also, if one deduces the situation correctly, a blessing which might well have been a curse, in that if the sending away is of primary importance to the spell-maker it could take on the character of a banishing spell, and a black one at that.

Another kind of binding spell involves the use of a gift. There are several ways of looking at this method of binding. The first is to regard the gift as containing within itself psychic forces which have been placed there either deliberately or involuntarily before it was given. An object which has been associated with acts of violence, or with religious and magical practices of some intensity, may, it is believed, retain energies released by those events. Thus we have many tales of "unlucky" jewels whose possessors always come to a bad end, and a large number of stories are based upon the notion that a "holy" object or jewel stolen from a shrine or statue will work against every owner of it until it is returned to its proper place. Certainly parapsychological experiments have shown that some objects do appear to contain some kind of energy totally unrelated to their physical properties. A second view is that a person may, as it were, impregnate a gift with psychic energies directed towards a particular purpose. Some black magicians plant such objects beneath the floors or on the thresholds of their enemies, and there are many recorded instances of illness and death following these plantings. In many of these cases the element of auto-suggestion is obviously present; the "gift" whose presence is known or suspected by the victim reinforces the destructive tendencies in his psyche. Thirdly, and perhaps most obviously, a gift can itself be a continual "message" to the deep mind of the owner: by means of inscriptions made upon it, or by means of its actual configuration, its symbolism, it can continually press home a message desired by the giver.

The power of the gift, as such, has always been recognized. The potlatch ceremonies of the Indians of the Pacific Northwest Coast of America, in which the host may give away almost all his wealth, are partly based upon the notion that to give to someone is to establish power over them until or unless they can, in time, give back more than they have received. Many anthropologists have stated that these potlatch ceremonies are rituals to establish status. This is certainly partly true. The speeches of the Kawakiutl at their potlatches, however, indicate that they also feel they have gained power. Several of these speeches are recorded by Ruth Benedict in her *Patterns of Culture*. Here are some of them; they were chanted by the host chief's retainers at these ceremonies. It is important to note that the speeches are in incantatory form, and that to many people an act of ridicule, a scorning, is also a magical act. It is said that the Ollavhs of ancient Ireland could raise warts and blotches on the skins of their opponents by means of ridicule. Thus to place oneself in the position of being able to ridicule someone without there being any chance of adequate response is, in fact, to place them in one's power, to bind them:

I am the great chief who makes people ashamed.
I am the great chief who makes people ashamed.
Our chief brings shame to the faces.

Our chief brings jealousy to the faces.

Our chief makes people cover their faces by what he is continually
doing in this world,

Giving again and again oil feasts to all the tribes.

I am the only great tree, I the chief!

I am the only great tree, I the chief!

You are my subordinates, tribes.

You sit in the middle of the rear of the house, tribes.

I am the first to give you property, tribes.

I am your Eagle, tribes!

Bring your counter of property, tribes, that he may try in vain
to count the property that is to be given away by the great
copper maker, the chief.

Go on, raise the unattainable potlatch-pole,

For this is the only thick tree, the only thick root of the tribes.

Now our chief will become angry in the house,

He will perform the dance of anger.

Our chief will perform the dance of fury.

Wa, out of the way,

Wa, out of the way.

Turn your faces that I may give way to my anger by striking my
fellow-chiefs.

They only pretend; they only sell one copper again and again
and give it away to the little chiefs of the tribes.

Ah, do not ask for mercy,

Ah, do not ask in vain for mercy and raise your hands, you with
lolling tongues.

I only laugh at him, I sneer at him who empties (the boxes of
property) in his house, his potlatch house, the inviting house
where we are made hungry.

I am the great chief who vanquishes,

I am the great chief who vanquishes.

Oh, go on as you have done!

Only at those who continue to turn around in this world,
Working hard, losing their tails (like salmon), I sneer,
At the chiefs under the true great chief.
Ha! have mercy on them! put oil on their dry brittle-haired heads,
The heads of those who do not comb their hair.
I sneer at the chiefs under the true great chief,
I am the great chief who makes people ashamed.[2]

This belief that power is gained over another by presenting him with gifts is also part of the make-up of so-called civilized man. There can hardly be any adult reader of this book who has not, at one time or another, given help to somebody and found that the person helped has thereafter felt "indebted" to such a degree as to lead him to sometimes violent acts of opposition. He has felt himself to be "in the power" of his benefactor, and has resented it. Some support for the "message-speaking" view of the gift is provided by the widespread custom of never allowing anyone to give another person a knife; the knife must be bought, usually with a small symbolic coin. Otherwise, it is supposed, the knife will cut the friendship with the recipient.

In almost all societies there are gift-giving ceremonies which include rituals which emphasize that either the gift is being made in the name of some power, spiritual or temporal, so that it cannot be regarded as giving one man power over another, or that the gift is blessed and consecrated, and that therefore no harm can come of it. We find these ceremonies occurring obviously at investitures, at marriages in many religious sects (the bride is "given away" in the Anglican Christian ceremonies), and even in the giving of names at baptismal and initiation ceremonies. We do not always recognize that behind some of our gift-giving there lies a desire to bind, to command if not servitude, then at least loyalty.

Some gifts, some bindings, carry with them explicit commands, as with the Ancient Irish *geasa*. The *geasa* is a command laid upon a person, by a person of priest-like or magical authority, which often involves a ban. Thus, in the legend of Deirdre, Fergus is under the spell of a *geasa*; he is obliged never to refuse hospitality, however awkward it may be. As a consequence his arrival at the house of Conchubor is too late to save the life of Naisi and his brothers. Other bans, and bindings, are laid upon members of religious sects. This man must not eat meat on Fridays. This man can only eat kosher food. This man must never have his head uncovered in a public place, and this woman must remain veiled whenever she is outside her own home. Such taboos are often, obviously, practical in origin; but they are also often indications that the person concerned is bound in fealty to a particular group or even a particular person.

This may seem to have taken us some way from the consideration of spells proper but it is, I think, important to approach the binding spell circuitously for it is very much a part of our living experience. Our contracts bind us, for example; our vows and oaths bind us. The oath we swear in courts of law is in essence a self-binding spell, and many oaths and vows contain an element of the *geasa* in that they say, "If I do not keep my word, then let me be destroyed or imprisoned." Here we touch upon the law of perjury, as well as upon the laws relating to breach of promise and breach of contract.

True binding and bidding spells are spells of power, and as such are often closely-guarded secrets. While anthropologists have collected many spells which are used communally, and are therefore common knowledge, they have collected very few power spells. Indeed, if one searches through any library of occult books one discovers that while the gathering of plants and other aspects of the physical ritual are often described in some detail, only occasionally does one find a complete verbal spell. The essential secret is withheld and handed down from generation to generation. There is a story of Alexander Carmichael, who was approached one morning by an old man who had permitted him the previous day to transcribe one of his spells. The old man begged Carmichael to burn his transcript—"for," he said, "that is the only wealth I have." Carmichael duly burned it. A Kwakiutl Indian chief told one of my friends, "Yes, we have many spells, but we do not tell them to anybody." A twentieth-century spell-maker I know has told me that some of her spells she will show to nobody. Similar secrecy surrounds initiation ceremonies in many societies ranging from the so-called "primitive" societies to masonic lodges, though the secrets have been revealed by dissidents in some instances. Spells of Power are rightly guarded; widespread knowledge of them might lead to misuse. Healing spells are also kept secret by many, for they are part of the spell-maker's "wealth," and, moreover, in the wrong hands a healing spell can easily be perverted into a harming spell. Hunting and gathering spells are less closely guarded, for it is in the general interest that as many people as possible be efficient food-providers. In societies where there are professional sorcerers, some spells become general knowledge, for the sorcerer is also a showman desirous of attracting attention to himself; nevertheless, even the professional sorcerer guards his most important spells and rituals, for otherwise he would simply be calling competitors into existence. All spell-makers know that the making of any spell involves a concentration and a psychic attitude which has to be learned over a period of time, like any art that involves more than practical dexterity.

Let us now turn to some examples of binding and bidding spells. As I have said, those concerned with hunting or plant-gathering are the most fully recorded, for they are of general importance to the community and are the least capable of being perverted to destructive ends. Here is a fishing spell from the Haoka of Guadalcanal in which the spell-maker first "binds" the fishing hook by describing it in terms of universal power, strength, and beauty, and then bids the fish to be caught by describing their capture. It concludes with an invocatory appeal to those who have previously owned and used the magic successfully, just as the Christianized spells of the Hebrides often end with an appeal to the "names" of power, and the Christian prayer ends with "in the name of the Father, the Son, and the Holy Ghost, So let it Be."

My pearl-shell hook is shining brightly.
It shines like the sun in the early morning across the sand,
Like the full moon striking the white of the reef,
Like phosphorescence dripping from the end of my paddles,
Like red flowers in the darkness of the forest.
My pearl-shell hook goes down into the water.

The fish from far away, from Aola and from Marau,
They see it and swim to look.
They struggle to enjoy it, fight one another to take it.
I pull them up—one, two, three, four, five—
So large nobody has seen their equal.
Nanama Riani, *nanama* Inonisondo
Tilani, Totovele, Sutu, Selo, Kikithia, Kuki,
Sasaka, Seka, Vonoa, Vuria, Kavora, Kapini,
Upolu, Ulua, Ngangenda, Ndambonoa, Tete, Vavasi,
Nanama, nanama, nanama.[3]

This spell is used together with a "vehicle;" it is described as

> a bundle of objects, generally of vegetable origin, chosen because
> of some real or fancied resemblance to the objective. The vehicle
> of the spell just quoted is made up of four vividly-coloured
> flowers and leaves; in beauty magic it consists of sweet-scented
> herbs; in gardening magic of the bark of several of the largest
> trees; in rain magic of the skin of melons and other juicy fruits.[4]

The Guadalcanal spell-maker is clearly using these objects as focusing or directional controls in the manner I have already discussed.
He also uses his breath in a special fashion, and makes appropriate
gestures:

> When he recites a spell he has ... to breathe hard on the
> vehicle and at the end of each line drench it with a fine spray of
> saliva. By this means the bundle of leaves or other objects
> becomes charged with vital force. The man places it in contact
> with whatever is to be influenced and is content to believe that
> he will now achieve what he wants. Sometimes, in addition, he
> is called upon to go through a pantomime. In magic for fishing,
> for instance, he makes the motion of hauling in a big catch; in
> magic to overcome fear he assumes a menacing attitude; in magic
> for beauty he pretends to stroke soft smooth flesh; and in that
> to cause sore feet he limps.[5]

The word *nanama* at the end of the spell is related to the word
Mana, used in many areas of the Pacific. This word signifies

spiritual or psychic power or energy, which can operate both for good and for evil. In the Pacific islands all excellence of mind or body, all good fortune in commerce or agriculture, in hunting or fighting, is explained in terms of *Mana*, a "lucky" person. Luck, like *Mana*, is not rationally explicable. You either have it or you don't.

This view of luck as spiritual power is shown in several gypsy spells.

If a man who is seeking for stolen goods finds willow twigs grown into a knot, he ties it up and says:

"I tie up the thief's luck!"

There is also a belief among the gypsies that these knots are twined by fairies, and that whoever undoes them undoes his own luck, or that of the person on whom he is thinking. These willow knots are much used in love-charms. To win the love of a maid, a man cuts one of them, puts it onto his mouth, and says:

"I eat thy luck,
I drink thy luck;
Give me that luck of thine,
Then thou shalt be mine."

Then the lover, if he can, secretly hides this knot in the bed of the wished-for bride.[6]

It is the spell-maker's object in many binding and bidding spells to bind good luck to him so firmly that success in any endeavour ceases to be a matter of chance. The binding has to be done carefully and in detail. We see this in many hunting songs. A good example is the well-known Navaho *Hunting Song*, in which the binding and bidding are fused together, the whole poem being an account of a successful hunt in which the speaker disguises himself as a blackbird so that the deer will be unafraid of him:

Comes the deer to my singing,
Comes the deer to my song,
Comes the deer to my singing.

He, the blackbird, he am I,
Bird beloved of the wild deer.
   Comes the deer to my singing.

From the Mountain Black,
From the summit,
Down the trail, coming, coming now,
   Comes the deer to my singing.

Through the pollen, flower pollen,
   Coming, coming now,
   Comes the deer to my singing.

Starting with his left fore-foot,
Stamping, turns the frightened deer,
   Comes the deer to my singing.

Quarry mine, blessed am I
In the luck of the chase.
   Comes the deer to my singing.

   Comes the deer to my singing,
   Comes the deer to my song,
   Comes the deer to my singing.[7]

The disguise element in this spell is not unique. The spell-maker may send his "message" by means of a disguise, by stating that he is a person or object that the subject of the spell either does not fear or actually likes. Like the Navaho songs, these are largely songs to gain access or acceptance, and are not infrequently used in love-spells. Such spells may involve the element of gift-bringing. Maurice Bowra records a song in which the Eskimo, "with a fine disregard for proprieties, offers to the caribou the shoes which he hopes to make from his skin and the lamp-wicks which he hopes to feed with its blubber."

Wild caribou, land-louse, long-legs,
With the great ears
And the rough hairs on your neck,
Flee not from me.

Here I bring skins for soles,
Here I bring moss for wicks;
Just come gladly,
Hither to me, hither to me.[8]

Sometimes the binding and bidding are fused in terms of a simple
series of commands, the commands themselves being regarded as
binding because they pattern exactly either the subject of the spell
or the event desired, as in the Vedda spell which is placed upon the
hunting arrow:

Go and drop behind the body of the monitor-lizard;
Pierce it, dear cousin.

Leave that place, arrow-brother,
Go and cleave it in the edge of the back.

Leave that place, arrow-brother,
Go and cleave it twice in the tail.

Leave that place, arrow-brother,
Go and cleave it twice in the neck.

Leave that place, arrow-brother,
Go and cleave it twice in the belly.

Leave that place, arrow-brother,
Go and fix yourself in the middle of the armpit.[9]

Other hunting spells take the opposite line and say nothing of the
desired event at all, but simply bind the creature to be hunted by
characterizing it and bringing it, as it were, into the hunter's
presence. Thus the Osage tribe of Plains Indians have the following Buffalo song:

I rise, I rise,
I, whose tread makes the earth to rumble.

I rise, I rise,
I, in whose thighs there is strength.

I rise, I rise,
I, who whips his back with his tail when in rage.

I rise, I rise,
I, in whose humped shoulder there is power.

I rise, I rise,
I who shakes his mane when angered.

I rise,
I whose horns are sharp and curved.[10]

Another tribe, or another spell-maker, might choose to make the implicit explicit by concluding the spell with the lines:

I rise, I rise,
I who accept the deep arrow.

In looking over spells of this and of other kinds one often notices that the actual intent is not made explicit. It is implied. This is, I believe, for two main reasons. The first is that it is always the concentrated intent, the psychic intensity which the person gives the message which carries the *Mana*. This intent need not be verbalized if the spell-maker himself, or herself, feels the spell to be effective without such explicit instruction. The second is that spell-makers are frequently disinclined to make their spells totally intelligible to outsiders. The buffalo spell just quoted could, indeed, simply appear to be a "poem" about buffalo. And many such "poems" and "songs" have been recorded without their magical intentions being understood.

Sometimes a spell may include or end with nonsense words which are the spell-maker's personal language for expressing his fundamental intent, and which carry the main psychic force of the message. In many cases this is the spell-maker's defence against others being able to use his spell effectively. Though it may be made, chanted, or, as most anthropologists say, "recited," in public and therefore become common knowledge, the essential part of it is kept secret by these means. Other secretive devices may involve the magical objects which the spell-maker may keep hidden in his medicine bag while sending his messages; even if the contents of the bag become known, the precise way in which those contents "speak" is known only to the spell-maker or to those to whom he has taught this language. This accounts for the apparently rather slapdash way in which some medicine bags appear to have been filled. Anthropologists have noted that "eye of newt and toe of frog" may be replaced by a dry leaf and a piece of bone by different spell-makers, who are yet probably intent upon the same ends. In fact some medicine bags or supposed magical amulets appear to be downright silly. But if the spell-maker is able to work satisfactorily with a Coke-bottle cap and a couple of buttons it does not mean that he is less competent or sophisticated or learned than someone whose medicine bag is filled with more bizarre objects and rarities. Nor is it true that the spell-maker or sorcerer who makes use of special clothing or implements is any more advanced than one who performs in ordinary working clothes. Each spell-maker has his or her own codes and formal necessities.

I have now reached a matter which I find difficult to discuss, yet I feel I cannot entirely avoid it. This is the Binding and Bidding spell intended to work upon other human beings for purposes other than healing or sex. The difficulty here is that any spell which seeks to bind and force a person to act in a manner to which they are disinclined must not only be extremely powerful, but feeds the power-drive, the selfish (and therefore self-destructive) desires of the spell-maker. Anyone who has made such a spell or curse knows that the amount of psychic energy sent out, and therefore experienced also by the sender, can be enormous and frightening. Many spells of this kind, moreover, involve the invocation of so-called "spirits," "demons" or "ghosts," which can, if not most securely bound and if the spell-maker is not well protected, do a great deal of damage. The raising of such forces is one of the main subjects of the old magical books, and in them a great deal of attention is paid to the making of protective spells and rituals, and to the use of objects which have been invested with power. These magical activities are commonly regarded as a part of Ceremonial Magic or High Magic, whose purpose is often to solve metaphysical problems, but also often to give the spell-maker power. Such acts can release forces from within the psyche that once released cannot be controlled. The magic with which I am concerned does not deal in such matters, and does not utilize more than the necessary minimum of ritual or order to direct the message clearly.

Nevertheless, provided the intent is not selfish, and provided that the symbols and names of power used are entirely creative and non-destructive, and provided also that the spell-maker is totally and wholly convinced of all this, it is possible to make binding and bidding spells without danger. We do, indeed, make the approximations quite frequently—whenever we wish a thing intensely or call a person's name or face to mind and passionately desire them to do something which is for their own good or the mutual good. Here is a modern binding and bidding spell:

> I touch the inner soul
> of this man with my finger
>
> I send the heat of the *Mana*
> into his soul
>
> I burn out all the coldness
> I burn out the suspicion
> I burn out all the jealousy
> I burn
>
> all the poison up
> all the dead things up
>
> I burn through the shackles on love
>
> He is changed, he is changed.[11]

This bidding and binding act is not dangerous, for all the binding and the bidding is healing, and intended to increase the creative drive of the subject. If the subject resists this message, if he turns it back upon the sender, it will operate positively and to the good of the sender. Were it, however, to conclude, powerfully and commandingly,

> He is my bondsman

then resistance to the message could result in emotional distress and confusion in the recipient, and perhaps in damage to the spell-maker who would then be demanding or working for personal power. A recognition of this in the spell-maker could lead also to his recognizing that the "bondsman" line ran counter in intent to the blessing elements in the spell and should oblige the spell-maker to add the final message, which, while not countering the spell of the blessings, prevents it from being malign in effect; a further line might run:

and I release him

The act of release is often part of the binding spell, or a corollary to it. Once the binding and bidding process is completed in the case of a spell which attempts to change the attitudes, beliefs or acts of a person, then the spell-maker is in the position of the teacher, the guru, the saint, the spiritual master, who releases his pupil or disciple from the bondage of apprenticeship. It is to say, "I have given you knowledge and power; do with it what you will," and implies that the released apprentice should, if he or she follows the lessons learned, do good and teach wisdom.

There is no rule as to the images which are correct for any one kind of spell, except that they must be those that the deep mind of the spell-maker and of the subject can comprehend. So they tend to be simple, elemental, archetypal images, images that have impressed themselves indelibly upon the family and cultural history of the maker and the subject.

Fire is often used as an image in spells. In a spell to cure jealousy based on a traditional Strikarmani (venereal or sexual) magic spell of India we find it used effectively:

This jealous passion you feel I here and now destroy. I take your heart in my hands and squeeze it as I squeeze a bladder, and I expel it like air and send it away. I blow it away as wind blows away the fire. It is leaving, it has left, it is finished, it is no longer a part of you.[12]

This, like other Strikarmani spells, is a vulgarization of a spell in the *Atharva-Veda*; the original reads:

1. The first impulse of jealousy, moreover the one that comes after the first, the fire, the heart-burning, that we do waft away from thee.

2. As the earth is dead in spirit, in spirit more dead than the dead, and as the spirit of him that has died, thus shall the spirit of the jealous (man) be dead!

3. Yon fluttering little spirit that has been fixed into thy heart, from it the jealousy do I remove as air from a water-skin.[13]

Here the fire is swept away by the wind, or by the breath of the spell-maker. In another spell against jealousy from the *Atharva-Veda* it is quenched by water:

1. From folk belonging to all kinds of people from the Sindhu (Indus) thou hast been brought hither: from a distance, I ween, has been fetched the very remedy for jealousy.

2. As if a fire is burning him, as if the forest-fire burns in various directions, this jealousy of his do thou quench, as a fire (is quenched) with water.[14]

The performance of this spell is accompanied by the pouring of water, just as the performance of the earlier one was accompanied by the spell-maker blowing out fire held over the man's body, or, possibly, over an image of the man's body.

Many spells make use of the events of history or of myths, re-calling them less as invocations than as reminders to the deep mind. Thus Edward Field's reworking of an Eskimo spell from Knud Rasmussen runs:

O sea goddess Nuliajuk,
when you were a little unwanted orphan girl
we let you drown.
You fell in the water
and when you hung onto the kayaks, crying,
we cut off your fingers.
So you sank into the sea
and your fingers turned into
the innumerable seals

You sweet orphan Nuliajuk,
I beg you now
bring me a gift,
not anything from the land
but a gift from the sea,
something that will make a nice soup.
Dare I say it right out?
I want a seal!

You dear little orphan,
creep out of the water
panting on this beautiful shore,
puh, puh, like this, puh, puh,
O welcome gift
in the shape of a seal![15]

The request element in this spell is not an uncommon phenomenon. It appears in many bidding and binding spells. One explanation given is that the individual animal is really simply one emanation, one appearance, of the whole animal spirit, which is in no way diminished by the killing and eating of this one creature. Thus the spell is asking the spirit of seal to give of its store. Another explanation is what I call the "safety-net" technique. By this I mean that the element of request makes it clear that the spell is in no way intended to work counter to the existing impulses and desires of the subject, but rather to reinforce the particular desires which would lead to the event the spell-maker intends. In this way the spell-maker is in no danger of creating a situation of conflict and stress, or of acting in a destructive and selfish fashion. Many spells in the Hebrides conclude with such phrases as "If it be the will of the Lord so to do," just as many prayer-spells in Christian churches include such phrases as "according to Thy will." These may tend to lessen the force of the psychic message in that they imply doubt; but they also clarify or purify the intent of the message, which is not to dominate but to direct and persuade. Such "safety nets" are only necessary when the spell could be misdirected towards power for its own sake, towards entirely selfish ends. It has been said over and over again that power corrupts, and I would emphasize again that psychic power corrupts psychically, and sometimes even physically, if it is used for destructive or anti-creative purposes.

6

Love Spells

Even now
The night is full of silver straws of rain,
And I will send my soul to see your body . . .

Chauras

Love spells are of many kinds. Some of them, especially oriental ones, are bidding and binding spells in which the spell-maker seeks to get the subject into bed, and are candidly erotic. This is, of course, logical, for the binding part of the spell must describe the subject in sexual terms, and the bidding part must present a detailed pattern of the wished-for event. Some spells are invocations, calling upon the appropriate spirit or god to accomplish the spell-maker's desires. Many are incantatory, seeking to bring both the spell-maker and the subject of the spell to the right emotional pitch. Many spells are also poems, and perhaps a higher proportion of love-spells are poems than any other because of their lyricism and passion. Spells are, however, poems by coincidence rather than by necessity. A good spell may well be a dull or flawed poem. Love poems, on the other hand, are often spells whether their authors label them so or not. Consider the following poem by Theodore Roethke, which he has called a "wish" rather than a "spell" or "charm:"

Wish for a Young Wife

My lizard, my lively writher,
May your limbs never wither,
May the eyes in your face
Survive the green ice
Of envy's mean gaze;
May you live out your life
Without hate, without grief,
And your hair ever blaze,
In the sun, in the sun,
When I am undone,
When I am no one.[1]

This is a Blessing rather than a Bidding or Binding poem. The Strikarmani magic of India is, however, largely devoted to binding and bidding. Here is a strong spell, even a brutal one, from the *Atharva-Veda*:

1. May (love) the disquieter, disquiet thee; do not hold out upon thy bed! With the terrible arrow of Kama (love) do I pierce thee in the heart.

2. The arrow, winged with longing, barbed with love, whose shaft is undeviating desire, with that, well-aimed, Kama shall pierce thee in the heart.

3. With that well-aimed arrow of Kama which parches the spleen, whose plume flies forward, which burns up, do I pierce thee in the heart.

4. Consumed by burning ardour, with parched mouth, do thou (woman) come to me, pliant, (thy) pride laid aside, mine alone, speaking sweetly and to me devoted!

5. I drive thee with a goad from thy mother and thy father, so that thou shalt be in my power, shalt come up to my wish.

6. All her thoughts do ye, O Mitra and Varuna, drive out of her! Then, having deprived her of her will, put her into my power alone![2]

The ritual accompanying this spell involves three days and nights of activity. Significantly, it concludes with the piercing of a clay figure through the heart with an arrow that has a point made of thorn, a shaft of black ala-wood, and a flight made from owls' feathers. In this image of the arrow West and East are at one; the arrow-pierced heart has been a feature of stories, legends, and poems about love in the West ever since the days of Greek civilization.

In this love spell there is no element of invocation until the very end, and even there it appears to be almost perfunctory. The spell-maker trusts in his own psychic power to direct the message with the required efficiency. Other spells invoke the assistance of spirits from the beginning and recall myths and historical events to bring power, as in the following two spells used by women to secure the love of men:

1. From thy head unto thy feet do I implant love's longing into thee. Ye gods, send forth the yearning love: may yonder man burn after me!

2. Favour this (plan), Anumati; fit it together, Akuti! Ye gods, send forth the yearning love: may yonder man burn after me!

3. If thou dost run three leagues away, (or even) five leagues, the distance coursed by a horseman, from there thou shalt again return, shalt be the father of our sons![3]

1. This yearning love comes from the Apsaras, the victorious, imbued with victory. Ye gods, send forth the yearning love: may yonder man burn after me.

2. My wish is, he shall long for me, devoted he shall long for me! Ye gods, send forth the yearning love: may yonder man burn after me!

3. That yonder man shall long for me, (but) I for him never-more, ye gods, send forth the yearning love: may yonder man burn after me!

4. Do ye, O Maruts, intoxicate him; do thou, O Agni, intoxicate him! May yonder man burn after me.[4]

It is noticeable that in Strikarmani magic the emphasis is placed firmly upon sexual desire. Many of these spells are accompanied by special rites, and by the creation of talismans which may or may not be given to the desired one for him or her to wear, often as a pendant, sometimes as another form of decoration. The giving of love-potions, as distinct from presumed aphrodisiacs, is also frequent. Sometimes the spell itself is simple while the rite is complex; sometimes it is the other way around. This curiously simple one is hardly a spell at all:

> Stick on the head of a girl's or woman's bed, as near as possible to the place where her head rests, a piece of virgin parchment on which have already been written the names of Michael, Gabriel, Raphael. Invoke these three angels to inspire (here pronounce the name of the beloved) with a love for you equal to your own. That person will not be able to sleep without first thinking of you, and very soon love will dawn in her heart. [5]

There are many instances of what we might call pillow talismans and threshold talismans, where the spell-maker simply plants the talisman upon the threshold or beneath the pillow of the subject. The pillow talisman seems to involve the idea of teaching a person while they are asleep, something which has also been used by people experimenting with techniques of "brainwashing." Many folk tales contain stories of people being given commands while sleeping which they obey on waking up.

Amulets do not really come within the scope of this book, but love-spells so often include reference to them or to "binding" gifts that it is necessary to mention them. A typical love-spell involving the use of a herbal charm is the following:

> Bagful of *haldi*-roots
> Eye-girl lighting a lamp
> The dark girls, the fair girls
> Hold out their hands
> Go my strong strong charm
> Go my leaping charm
> Awake love in this girl
> Love in her walking feet
> Love in the dust her feet stir

Love in her seeing eyes
Love in her moving eyelids
Love in her listening ears.
Love in her laughing teeth
Awake, love my charm
Love in the breasts ready to be fondled
Love in the vagina fit for love
Go my strong strong charm
Let the charm take this girl.[6]

Sexual desire if often both possessive and jealous. The magicians of Malaysia seem to be particularly addicted to violent imagery and to combine the love charm with the curse, as in:

I would wed the image in the pupil of my mistress' eye
With the image in the pupil of my own!
If thou lookest not upon me
May thy eyeballs burst![7]

This combination of the binding and the curse, frequent in certain love-spells, also occurs in many other kinds of spell. It is an unwise form of spell to create, for the destructive element of the message may outweigh the constructive in intensity and bring disorder upon the spell-maker as well as, or instead of, the subject. Another strategy typical of Malaysian and of many Muslim spells is the use of conditional statement. This has always been a part of prophetic magic, and is well exemplified in Shakespeare's making the witches prophesy to Macbeth that he would be safe until Birnham wood came to Dunsinane, which, of course, it did. The Malaysian magician who created the following spell may have been fairly safe with her first line, but her second condition could easily be upset by land subsidence or an earth tremor. The imagery here is also strange, for it suggests less the passionate love of the man desired than the inactivity of the weary husband no longer interested in his wife's body.

If Muhammad can be sundered from Allah
And a corpse move in the grave,
Only then shall my lover's desire move to another.

The desire of his heart shall be only for me;
Straying now hither he shall be my mate until death
Safe near me like a corpse in the grave.[8]

A more active partner is envisaged by the magician who created the
next Malaysian spell, though here again (if the translation is to be
trusted) the beloved appears to be plagued rather than blessed with
love's fever. As in a number of spells from Muslim areas, the opening invocation seems to run somewhat counter to the tone of the
rest of the spell.

In the name of God, the Merciful, the Compassionate!
I fry sand from the footprint of my beloved;
Nay, I fry her heart and liver
Night and day, as this sand is fried.
"Let it be" says Allah.
"And it is so," says Muhammad, His Prophet.
Let her body itch with desire
Giving her no rest from longing for me.
"And it is so," says Gabriel.[9]

There is something predatory in a good many love-spells and love-
rituals, and their predatory nature does make them dangerous.
Nevertheless, perhaps partly because a great part of the world
entertains fantasies of sexual domination, love-spells (often of
dubious effectiveness) turn up in a good many books. One love-
spell which gives us an interesting variation upon the conditional
spell is the Hyacinth Spell.

Actually, this may be performed with any type of bulb from a
tulip to an onion! Habondia being the patroness of all flowers,
however, a sweet-smelling variety stands more chance of success,
I always feel.
Plant the bulb in a new pot, naming it as your loved one as
you do. Every morning and evening when you water it, chant
these words intently over it.

As this root grows
and this blossom blows,
may her heart be turned to me.
As my will, so mote it be![10]

The lover who is an inept gardener will clearly fail at this one.

A gypsy spell uses a willow tree in a similar fashion. In this case the girl follows the man she desires until he makes a clear footprint in the earth. She then digs out the earth which carries the footprint and buries it under a willow tree, saying,

Many earths on earth there be,
Whom I love my own shall be,
Grow, grow willow tree!
Sorrow none unto me!
He the axe, I the helve,
He the cock, I the hen,
This, this (be as) I will.[11]

The symbols of the axe and helve and of the cock and hen are also used in another love spell, worth including purely for its grotesque element (even Huson, who records it, clearly does not take it too seriously). It crudely combines sympathetic magic with the binding spell of the gift.

The ingredients for this sorcery are simply a bitch in heat and another, male dog, plus a small, attractive looking-glass such as the warlock knows will prove acceptable to the object of his lust. Now the trick of this spell lies in arranging that the two dogs couple on a Thursday around the hour of 8 AM, 3 PM, or 10 PM; having arranged for this accordingly, you must then contrive to catch the reflection of the copulating dogs in your looking glass, uttering this spell forcefully as you do so, and bending your basilisk gaze on the scene before you:

I the dog and she the bitch,
I the helve and she the axe,
I the cock and she the hen.
As my will, so mote it be!

Having done this, hopefully without exciting too much attention from your neighbors, either present the loaded looking glass to your future ladylove as a gift, or in some way induce her to gaze into it. One look and she will be lost to you. Be prepared to have the clothes torn from your back.[12]

Spells of this quality are clearly degenerate. That they are so freely bandied about, and that there is so much so-called "popular" writing on love-philtres, aphrodisiacs, and erotic strategy should perhaps make us immediately suspicious, though not perhaps as totally disbelieving as the advertisement I once saw for an aphrodisiac which had been labelled, in large headlines, *Placebo*. But from this last absurdity and from these other crude attempts to excite lust rather than sexually unifying love, we can see just how considerable an appeal the notion of love-magic makes to most of us. We can also see, because of the very crudity of many of these spells, the way in which the spell-maker, dominated by a complex emotion, is not always able to sort out the component parts of love and jealousy, desire and resentment of desire, and even lust and contempt. We can see in the dog spell a quite clear denigration of the very sexual ecstasy that is being demanded, and in the Malaysian spells a fury that though certainly lecherous is hardly amatory.

Perhaps the incantatory love-spell that describes the actions of lovers arouses the appropriate emotions without self-defeating complexity, at least in some. Lenore Kandel's once notorious *Love Book* contains material which, while not labelled as spells, certainly appears to be incantatory in intention as well as in mode.

to fuck with love—
to know the tremor of your flesh within my own—
    feeling of thick sweet juices running wild
    sweat   bodies tight and tongue to tongue

I am all those ladies of antiquity enamored of the sun
my cunt is a honeycomb we are covered with come and honey
we are covered with each other my skin is the taste of you

fuck—the fuck of love-fuck—the yes entire—
love out of ours—the cock in the cunt fuck—
the fuck of pore into pore—the smell of fuck
taste it—love dripping from skin to skin—
tongue at the doorways—cock god in heaven—
love blooms entire universe—I/you
reflected in the golden mirror we are avatars of Krishna and
     Radha
  pure love-lust of godhead   beauty unbearable
    carnal incarnate
I am the god-animal, the mindless cuntdeity   the hegod-
   animal
is over me, through me   we are become one total angel
united in fire   united in semen and sweat   united in
   lovescream

  sacred our acts and our actions
  sacred our parts and persons

sacred the sacred cunt!
sacred the sacred cunt!
miracle!   miracle!   sacred the primal miracle!
  sacred the god-animal, twisting and wailing
    sacred the beautiful fuck[13]

Here the erotic fantasy, as incantation, is well exemplified, and
here we may begin to see one of the main difficulties attending the
making of love-spells. It is, quite simply, that it is hard for any
person to tell the difference between the transmitting of psychic
energy and the self-energizing experience of sexual fantasy, perhaps because they can be very similar in effect as well as nature.

   The transmission of a psychic message is one thing; the self-
absorbed creation of a wish-fulfilling fantasy is another. In the first
case the intensity of the psychic drive is such as to exclude all other
considerations; in the second the sexual drive mobilizes energies
which prevent the psychic drive from achieving its full potential
and may even be, fundamentally, of such a narcissistic or auto-
erotic nature as to block transmission. It is possible that the most

effective love-spells are those transmitted at close quarters when the sexual drive itself awakes a sympathetic response in the other person, and when, therefore, only a very simple psychic message may be required. The love-spell that reinforces an already existing or stirring desire in the subject, and therefore is not obliged to emphasize the binding element, can be as effective as any other kind. There are a number of these in the writings of poets of the Middle East. This one, by the nineteenth-century Afghan poet Muhammad Din Tilai, is reminiscent of the Navaho hunting spell in its use of repetition:

Come, my beloved! And I say again: Come, my beloved!
The doves are moaning and calling and will not cease.
   Come, my beloved!

"The fairies have made me queen, and my heart is love.
Sweeter than the green cane is my red mouth."
   Come, my beloved!

The jacinth has spilled odour on your hair,
The balance of your neck is like a jacinth;
You have set a star of green between your brows.
   Come, my beloved!

Like lemon-trees among the rocks of grey hills
Are the soft colours of the airy veil
To your rose knee from your curved almond waist.
   Come, my beloved!

Your light breast veil is tawny brown with stags,
Stags with eyes of emerald, hunted by red kings.
   Come, my beloved!

Muhammad Din is wandering; he is drunken and mad;
For a year he has been dying. Send for the doctor!
   Come, my beloved![14]

Here the girl is described and therefore "bound;" the spell loses some of its energy, but not much, in its last verse by the spell-maker's reflecting upon his own condition. This spell is almost no more than persuasive poetry, like most love poems, which are intended to persuade by their expressions of need and of love rather than command by means of their psychic power. Sometimes it is hard to tell the difference. Indeed, the only difference between them may be the intensity with which the spell-maker or poet performs his words and the emphasis or interpretation he places upon particular words and phrases. Another poem, from *The Thousand and One Nights*, is more obviously a spell proper:

O Lord, who made her lips as honey sweet
Yet sharper than the sickle in the wheat,
    Grant me to be the honey to her steel,
O Lord, who made her to mow down the wheat;
    O Lord, make me the carpet of her heel,
Who make the dream above her visiting feet.

O Lord, who cast the fullness of her hips
And made her spittle more than raisin drips,
    Favour the onyx tears I weep for her,
O Lord, who made her as the rain drips.

O Lord, who made her roses on a stem
With golden starlight shining on to them,
    Grant that those roses pierce me to the heart,
O Lord, who made the starlight smile on them.

O Lord, who sent her as a silver mole
To fret my heart and tear into my soul,
    May she return to ravage them again,
O Lord, who made the body and the soul.[15]

In most cases the love-spell dwells upon the physical beauty of the person desired. In some it deals with the physical manifestations of desire, as in the anonymous twentieth-century spell:

Thinking of me
    let her lips be soft
Thinking of me
    let her palms be moist
Thinking of me
    let her nipples be stiff

Thinking of me
    let her loin be wet
Let her think of me,
Let her think of me,
Asleep and Awake let her
think of me.[16]

This is a spell to arouse desire, but not necessarily love. There are
many spells to increase virility or cure impotence. A spell from the
Atharva-Veda begins with the digging up, with an iron plough-
share, of the root of *feronia elephantum* or of *mucuna puritus*, and
with the words,

Bulls have dug thee up, thou art a bull, O herb! thou art a bull,
full of lusty force; in behalf of a bull do we dig thee up!

The plants are bruised and steeped in water and the infusion is
mixed with milk. The spell-maker then seats himself with a drawn
bow in his lap and performs the spell. He may also, or alternatively,
seat himself upon a stake or pestle or other phallic shaped object.
The spell runs:

1. Thee, the plant, which the Gandharva dug up for Varuna,
when his virility had decayed, thee, that causes strength, we
dig up.

2. Ushas (Aurora), Surya (the sun), and this charm of mine;
the bull Pragapati (the lord of creatures) shall with his lusty
fire arouse him!

3. This herb shall make thee so very full of lusty strength,
that thou shalt, when thou art excited, exhale heat as a thing on
fire!

4. The fire of the plants and the essence of the bulls shall
arouse him! Do thou, O Indra, controller of bodies, place the
lusty force of men into this person!

5. Thou (O herb) art the first-born sap of the waters and
also of the plants. Moreover thou art the brother of Soma and
the lusty force of the antelope buck!

6. Now, O Agni, now, O Savitar, now, O goddess Saras-
vati, now, O Brahmanaspati, do thou stiffen the pasas as a bow!

7. I stiffen thy pasas as a bowstring upon the bow. Embrace thou (women) as the antelope buck the gazelle with ever unfailing (strength)!

8. The strength of the horse, the mule, the goat and the ram, moreover the strength of the bull bestow upon him, O controller of bodies (Indra)![17]

Many love spells involve the giving or taking of potions. It seems that when the spell is intended to affect a bodily appetite it is necessary to feed the body actually as well as symbolically. This is not always so with spells intended to cause sexual attraction. It appears to be assumed that in all but special cases sexual excitement will lead to appropriate physical consequences in both men and women. Nevertheless, perhaps because love magic is especially difficult to control, a greater number of love spells are accompanied by rituals than are any other type.

For some reason a larger number of love-charms are accompanied by specific rituals than any other type. This Gaelic love charm is basically a recipe for an act of ritual magic rather than a spell in itself:

A love charm for thee,
Water drawn through a straw,
The warmth of him (her) thou lovest,
    With love to draw on thee.

Arise betimes on Lord's day,
To the flat rock of the shore
Take with thee the pointed canopy,
    And the cap of a priest.

A small quantity of embers
In the skirt of thy kirtle,
A special handful of sea-weed
    In a wooden shovel.

Three bones of an old man,
Newly torn from the grave,
Nine stalks of royal fern,
    Newly trimmed with an axe.

Burn them on a fire of faggots
And make them all into ashes;
Sprinkle in the fleshy breast of thy lover,
    Against the venom of the north wind.

Go round the "rath" of procreation,
The circuit of the five turns,
And I will vow and warrant thee
    That man (woman) shall never leave thee.[18]

The twentieth-century love-spell maker has problems that did not trouble his forebears. Woman is no longer a chattel, and, in most of western civilization, has chosen not to be regarded as either a goddess (religious or magical power-source) or a sex object. Moreover the simplicities of early eroticism are no longer adequate to describe the desires and satisfactions of men and women in our complex society. The "cave-man" approach of some of the Malaysian magicians is definitely out, because the spell-maker himself, or herself, can no longer easily send that message, can no longer treat the subject of the spell with that simple assurance with which the Indian spell-maker can treat the deer. And yet the spell must still be in that near-timeless and simple language of symbols and commands which carries the message effectively and authoritatively to the deep mind, which remains relatively unaffected by the shifts in social fashion. While the composer of the Vedic spells or believers in Mohammedan and other religious and mythological traditions could use images of power which carried conviction equally to the conscious and the deep mind, the twentieth-century spell-maker is frequently working outside such orthodoxies. Nevertheless, he is usually aware of the symbols which most affect the deep mind because of his own personal experience of dreams and nightmares, and because he still recalls the symbols which excited him in childhood. Consequently he can overcome the problems presented to him by his cultural environment and produce spells as direct, powerful, and simple as those of any older spell-maker. It is interesting to compare the Strikarmani spell for virility already given with a twentieth-century spell with the same intention. The latter is less allusive and more direct in speech. It is a self-blessing spell.

126

Great Ash,
Holy Ash,
Broad-spreading Ash Tree,
As your twigs thicken with Spring,
As your great buds swell
And burst the foam of their ecstasies,
O Great Ash,
So strengthen and accomplish
This my desire.[19]

The Ash, while not being decorated within the spell itself by any precise reference to its attributes, is regarded as a Chieftain by the Brehon Laws of ancient Celtdom. Robert Graves, in *The White Goddess*, says that its nobility is justified by "its timber, used for supporting the King's thigh ... and for the shafts of weapons."[20] In this spell, the message exerts its energy effectively by the directness of its speech as well as by its utilization of an age-old symbol known consciously to be appropriate. As rational thought excludes psychic passion, it is obvious that either the critical and logical mind has to be entirely excluded and even denied, or that it has to be so totally in agreement with the message that it is entirely subordinated to it and gives up its claim upon the spell-maker.

The symbols of love-spells should be those which arouse sensations of creative strength, should be images of growing and images which send messages of life's vitality. Thus many love-spells and love poems utilize the vocabulary of growing things, as does the following spell, which also uses a "tree language:"

Alder of suppleness
Lay her supple beside me
Red-lipped Elder
Let her rejoice in my kiss
Smooth-skinned Madrona
Slide naked her arms around me
Red-stemmed Dogwood
Hurry her veins with fire[21]

Like many spells, this one can be altered to the requirements of the individual by changing "her" to "him." Indeed, many spell-makers change existing spells either by refining or changing their direction, or by adding words and phrases which make them their own. Unless the message is felt to be entirely personal and unique it is unlikely that the psychic energy will be particularly powerful.

Many love-spells are, as we have seen, binding spells. Some, however, are best described as "beckoning" rather than "binding." The spell-maker does not wish to enslave, to have power over his subject, but to bring him or her willingly and eagerly to the place and time for love. This poem by Rabindranath Tagore is a beckoning spell. It is worth noticing that the only true "binding" element is that which "binds" or controls all possible impediments to the poet's lover coming, and that the time of day is indicated to ensure that the person beckoned will come at the prescribed hour and not at any other:

Come as you are; do not loiter over
your toilet.
If your braided hair has loosened, if
the parting of your hair be not straight,
if the ribbons of your bodice be not
fastened, do not mind.
  Come as you are; do not loiter over your toilet.

  Come, with quick steps over the
grass.
  If the raddle come from your feet
because of the dew, if the rings of bells
upon your feet slacken, if pearls drop
out of your chain, do not mind.
  Come, with quick steps over the
grass.

  Do you see the clouds wrapping the
sky?
  Flocks of cranes fly up from the
further river-bank and fitful gusts of
wind rush over the heath.

The anxious cattle run to their stalls
in the village.

Do you see the clouds wrapping the
sky?

In vain you light your toilet lamp
—it flickers and goes out in the wind.

Who can know that your eyelids
have not been touched with lamp-
black? For your eyes are darker
than rain-clouds.

In vain you light your toilet lamp—
it goes out.

Come as you are; do not loiter over your toilet.

If the wreath is not woven, who
cares; if the wrist-chain has not been
linked, let it be.

The sky is overcast with clouds—it is
late.

Come as you are; do not loiter over
your toilet.[22]

Such "beckoning" spells, or near-spells, are very common indeed.
They are often simply extensions of that telepathic non-verbal
message-sending which occurs between people who are psychically
in tune with one another. Tagore's spell, however, introduces the
element of time, and this deserves a comment. Most binding spells
do not specify a time, for there is no need. To be bound is to be
bound, and that is all there is to it. But beckoning spells and other
love-spells often have a time attached. There are two reasons for
this. One is obvious—there seems little point in having your beloved
turn up at your bedroom door when you are away on vacation. The
other is that some spell-makers find it effective to state a particular
time in the spell so that the message "hits," reaches its climax of
power, at a precise moment. It is a way of concentrating the
message. Wise spell-makers who put a time-element in their spells
will, however, be practical about it. At some times of day the
psychic message may have to overcome long-standing habits of eat-

ing, sleeping, or bathing, or conflict with other elements in a person's timetable. This conflict may well result in the psychic message being ignored or dismissed as unimportant. Spell-makers who are astrologers or numerologists sometimes work out the appropriate hour, but even most numerologists and astrologers are a little dubious as to the accuracy of their sciences in evaluating short spaces of time. This spell plays safe–unless, of course, the beloved works a night shift:

> It is a midnight
> my hand is touching yours
> your lips are parted
> my mouth is touching yours
> It is midnight
> my name shines in your mind
> And your body trembles
> It is midnight.[23]

The simplicity of this deserves a comment. On the whole, the simpler the spell the more effective it will be, and this is particularly true of love-spells. One reason for this is that most spell-makers, unless their concentration is so intense as to put them in a trance, in which they will have extraordinary stamina, cannot keep up the psychic power for very long at a time. Another reason is that the longer the spell the more likelihood there is of its being flawed by lapses of attention and consequent inaccuracies. Eric Maple gives the texts of two very short love spells. He says:

> In the South Pacific young girls in quest of a mate chanted the following words as a magical lure to men:

>> Man you are behind me,
>> You follow me. You want me.
>> You come from behind to me,[24]

He also tells of

> the courtship customs of the Australian aborigine, who traces an outline of the woman he desires in the sand with his spear and hopefully sings his magic song:

>> Long string make her like me
>> Long string make her like me.[25]

These are typical of the love-spells still in use in unsophisticated societies, both in their brevity and their simplicity. Many spell-makers rather than write a long spell make a series of short ones, each adding something to the message of its predecessors or qualifying and making more definite the overall message. Sometimes it is only at the end of making such a series and after an hour or more of concentrated and exhausting labour that the spell-maker will know that his message has been received and that the spell is working. Spells made in series, however, must not contradict each other in intent. This is obvious. Nor should they differ too widely in their method, for each method uses a slightly different "wavelength."

The most honest and perhaps the most effective love-spell is the spell of blessing for a loved one. It may not arouse desire; that is not its intent. It may not bring him or her to your side; that is not its plan. It will, however, if the blessing is wholehearted, ease its object of those anxieties, tensions, and fears which may be obstacles between you and will make him or her receptive to your other psychic messages. It is important to realize that in this genre of spells, as in all others, the message will be most potent if the subject is in a receptive condition, however that condition may have been attained. Here is a spell I made myself:

Let in the clear,
let in the bright
that my love meet
her dream tonight.

Let in the smooth,
let in the warm
that sleep may keep
my love from harm.

Let in the moon,
let in the stars
to watch my love
through these still hours.

Let in the peace,
let in the peace
that all my love's
long sadness cease.[26]

7

Healing Spells

> *"It is not only the body that by its
> sound constitution strengthens
> the soul, but the well-regulated soul
> by its authoritative power maintains
> the body in perfect health"*

Plato

Any discussion of spells of healing is bound to meet with scepticism and even opposition from many people who distrust so-called faith-healers and who believe, with complete justification, that much human suffering has been caused to many people by their placing their health entirely in the hands of unorthodox medical practitioners. It must therefore be emphasized, first of all, that all sensible makers of healing spells also advise their subjects to seek the help of doctors and that some will not even attempt a healing spell for some disorders unless orthodox medicine has already been tried and found ineffective. On the other hand almost all doctors will agree that healing spells do work, and sometimes with quite astonishing effectiveness. I have known doctors who have been unable to cure warts advise patients to have them "charmed away," and in many cases the spells have been entirely successful. Doctors are also aware of self-induced or psychosomatic diseases, and many therefore believe that psychosomatic healing can and does occur. In some instances where a disorder is suspected to be of psychosomatic origin the doctor may advise that the patient visit a psychiatrist, and especially one adept in hypnotic techniques. Few doctors discount the effectiveness of faith-healing; almost all have observed sudden and inexplicable remissions of very severe diseases, and almost all have observed cures they cannot explain. In many instances doctors have changed their diagnosis of a disorder after the unexpected and inexplicable cure has occurred; politicians are not the only people who deal in wisdom after the event.

On the whole, though, doctors regard faith-healing, healing spells and the like with disfavour, for all too often the spell-maker or faith-healer, inadequately informed as to the heart of the matter, may succeed in clearing up a symptom without dealing with its cause, and thus delude the patient and do nothing to slow down the progress of the disease. Even in cases where auto-suggestive techniques involving hypnosis and even hysteria may bring temporary relief, that relief may be short-lived. If the patient then returns to the faith-healer rather than the doctor the results may be disastrous. On the other hand, while the cautious and sceptical view of the doctor is justified, the spell-maker's doubts about orthodox medicine are often equally well-founded. There are many instances of doctors advocating unnecessary surgery, sometimes of an "exploratory" kind, when a psychosomatic cure has been possible. I myself have known cases where surgery has been planned and then cancelled because the patient has been given relief or even wholly cured by a spell-maker.

All this leads to the warning that anyone attempting healing spells should be very careful to get, somehow or other, as full a diagnosis as possible of the disorder he is treating. Some spell-makers are also students of homeopathic medicine, which helps the body cure itself by means of minuscule reinforcements of its natural urge to make itself whole. This is closer to the thinking of their philosophy than that of the medical practitioners who bludgeon the body with massive doses of antibiotics and formidable vaccines. Here, the spell-maker of today is only following a long-established tradition. The Wise Women of the past, some of whom were burned as witches, were almost all learned in the medicinal and hallucinogenic properties of herbs and roots. Most of them, indeed, appear to have combined healing spells with medical treatment, and while later research suggests that some of the treatment was more a psychological reinforcement of the subject's will to be healed than a cure by any other means, we must appreciate that various forms of placebo are used widely in modern medicine also.

Healing spells are governed by much the same rules as all other spells, and may involve invocation, incantation, and binding and bidding, with or without accompanying rituals or arrangements of selected objects that establish "hot lines" between the spell-maker and the subject. The main difference between healing spells and others is that actual personal contact between the spell-maker and the subject is more frequent. Moreover a great many of them are also accompanied by the administration of "medicine" to the sufferer. Some of this medicine, though seemingly both ludicrous and primitive, does in fact have actual pharmaceutical effects. Many of the poultices suggested by the "Wise Women," "Magicians," "Sorcerers" and "Witch Doctors" have curative properties whose value has been discovered by later researchers and frequently used in the making up of various drugs. Some of the "medicine," though, is equally clearly of the placebo or message-intensifying kind, and functions solely to give the patient confidence in the power and efficacy of the healing. Some medicine of this kind derives from the simplest form of sympathetic magic. But no matter what the rituals or medicines that accompany them, the spells themselves follow the patterns already described in other chapters, and use the same verbal techniques.

One of the most common healing spells is that which uses names of power in a description of previous acts of healing, as in the *Charm for the Sprain* included in *Carmina Gadelica*:

Bride went out
In the morning early,
With a pair of horses;
One broke his leg,
With much ado,
That was apart,
She put bone to bone,
She put flesh to flesh,

> She put sinew to sinew,
> She put vein to vein;
> As she healed that
> May I heal this.[1]

A similar use of historical or mythical reference can be seen in this Swedish spell:

> Dave rode across a bridge
> When he came to Tive Wood,
> His horse tripped over a root,
> twisted a foot.
> Odin came by:
> "I will cure the twist
> of bone, flesh, and limb.
> Your foot will not ache
> and never more break.
> +++ Amen.[2]

Here we have, once again, a kind of cultural inconsistency in that Odin makes the sign of the cross three times and says "Amen." Some of these anecdotal spells are notable for brevity, and remind one more of children's rhymes than of anything else–for instance, this spell against snake bites:

> Jesus and Peter walked down the road.
> Peter said: The snake bit
> Maria came with her tiny keys
> and hit the bite: SKAT![3]

This would, presumably, be accompanied by a clapping of the hands or a light blow on the wound itself.

The same type of spell is also to be found in gypsy lore. A gypsy spell against the toothache runs:

> Peter was sitting on a marble stone,
> And Jesus passed by.
> Peter said, "My Lord, my God,
> How my tooth doth ache!"
> Jesus said, "Peter thou art whole!

136

And whosoever keeps these words for My sake
Shall never have the toothache."[4]

This is a charm; the words are to be written down and carried on the body of the person who wishes protection.

This kind of spell no longer carries much conviction; it is too simple and anecdotal. On the other hand many faith-healers of a Christian persuasion use a similar method. By preliminary and incantatory reference to Christ's miracles, followed by an invocation to Christ, they establish the power of the message that they are sending "in the name of Jesus" before either laying on hands or commanding the patient to be cured.

A spell method not used by most religious healers is the bidding spell involving ridicule, which consists largely of the command for the illness to go, together with some animadversions upon what one might almost call the moral character of the affliction and its unwelcomeness. Such spells are common in the tackling of disorders of the skin, such as warts, pimples, and styes. A Pennsylvanian German spell to banish a stye commands, accuses and punishes with great force and brevity:

Stye, thou corruptest N.N.'s blood
Therefore I take away thy goods.
God help thee N.N.[5]

Two even simpler and more directly insulting remedies are for warts. We are told, "Call a wart on a cow's udder 'fig' and it will disappear," and, "Call a wart on a horse 'asche' and it will disappear."[6] The number of spells and remedies for curing warts is almost countless. In many cases the spell is either a straightforward banishing spell, often involving mockery, or an equally straightforward cleansing spell, as in the simple:

Let the hand be clean
Let the skin be smooth
Let the skin be soft
Let the hand be pure.[7]

Many wart-charmers do not even concern themselves with verbalizing the message. They simply visualize, with intensity, the absence of the wart and the cleanness of the patient's skin; while a bad case may need several repetitions, the warts usually disappear.

Some charms and spells make use of the "timing" element I mentioned earlier. A simple wart cure, again from the Pennsylvanian Germans, is to stroke the wart while looking through the window at the new moon, and

> Say the following three times in succession ... "What I see, increase; what I touch, decrease." On the third day of the new moon, take the patient out into the open, put your finger on the warts, and looking at the new moon, say: "What I see increases; what I touch decreases." Say this three times in succession and then go indoors.[8]

Sometimes warts are cured by "selling" them, "giving them away," or by transferring them to another person. There are many healing spells in which the disease is transmitted to some other place. Sometimes it is transferred to an object which is then buried or destroyed or placed in a particular and perhaps holy place. Sometimes it is transferred deliberately to a passing stranger. Sometimes the healer himself "takes on" the disease, which he is strong enough to withstand and banish from himself once he possesses it. This giving away of disease can still be seen in a residual form in those children's games of "tag" or "tig," in which the object is to touch another person and then avoid him; if he or she touches you, then you will become an outcast. This clearly also has its origins in simple notions of contagion as well as in a deep-seated belief that touching constitutes the sending of a message, a transference of good or malign energy. A Gaelic charm for the removal of a mote from the eye exists in many versions.

> The reciter, Isabel Calder, crofter, Tulloch, Bonar Bridge, Sutherland, says that she got the power of the Eye Charm from her father Finlay Calder.
> Her father was famous throughout his district for his occult powers. Without personal contact with the sufferer, he could remove a mote from the eye and stop bleeding; he could also

cure chest-contraction. All these cures he performed many times, never unsuccessfully. He always prayed that the mote in the eye might be placed upon his tongue, and this always happened. On one occasion, however, he found that the mote which was removed from the eye to his tongue was an insect. From the disgust this caused him he contracted jaundice. After this he prayed the great God of life to place the mote from the eye upon his hand, instead of upon his tongue, and this always happened. The reciter gave many examples, from her father's experience and from her own, of the removal of the mote by means of occult powers. These mysterious manifestations are beyond the writer's power to explain.

Finlay Calder is spoken of throughout his district as a good man, and as a good Christian of marvellous miracles. He died at the age of seventy-two years. How he exercised such powers no one can explain, but the people of his district explicitly maintain that he did so.

The reciter says that she herself always feels a bitter, disagreeable taste in her mouth after performing the cure.

Place, Thou King of peace,
Place, Thou Christ of the cross,
  Place, Thou guiding Spirit,
This mote upon my palm.

The King be by my palm,
Christ be by my foot,
  The guiding Spirit be by my knee,
The eye be at rest.

Grant, Thou King of the eyes,
Grant, Thou Christ of the cross,
  Grant, Thou guiding Spirit,
Calm to the eye this night.

  In name of the King of life,
  In name of the Christ of love,
  In name of the Spirit Holy,
    Triune of peace.[9]

Some Gaelic healers used the transferring spell for Chest Seizure, as in the following:

I will heal thee,
　Mary will heal with me,
Mary and Michael and Brigit
　Be with me all three.

Thy strait and thy sickness
　Be upon the earth holes,
Be on the grey stones,
　Since they have firmest base.

Be upon the birds of the sky,
　Be upon the wasps of the knolls,
Be upon the whales of the sea,
　Since they have swiftest body.

Be upon the clouds of the skies,
　Since they are pronest to rain,
Be upon the stream of the river
　Whirling to the wave.[10]

A gypsy spell of this kind is accompanied by medication. To cure pain in the eyes, the spell-maker washes them with a mixture of spring or well water and saffron while saying:

Oh, pain from the eyes
Go into the water
Go out of the water
Into the saffron,
Go out of the saffron
Into the earth.
To the Earth-Spirit.
There's thy home.
There go and eat.[11]

Another spell against pain, this time incantatory:

Power of moon have I over thee,
　Power of sun have I over thee,

Power of rain have I over thee,
    Power of dew have I over thee,
Power of sea have I over thee,
    Power of land have I over thee,
Power of stars have I over thee,
    Power of planets have I over thee,
Power of universe have I over thee,
    Power of skies have I over thee,
Power of saints have I over thee,
    Power of heaven have I over thee,
Power of heaven and power of God have I over thee,
    Power of heaven and power of God over thee.

A part of thee on the grey stones,
A part of thee on the steep mountains,
A part of thee on the swift cascades,
A part of thee on the gleaming clouds,
A part of thee on the ocean-whales,
A part of thee on the meadow-beasts,
A part of thee on the fenny swamps,
A part of thee on the cotton-grass moors,
    A part on the great surging sea—
        She herself has best means to carry,
            The great surging sea,
        She herself has best means to carry.[12]

A charm to cure the "prickly sleep" (sometimes called "pins and needles") in a child's foot shows that at least in some instances the transferring spell was known to be a way of conveying the right message to a patient who believed that a disorder had to go somewhere, and could not just vanish. Here the actual cure for "pins and needles" is given in the spell, for the child is made to walk until the blood is circulating properly once again:

Prickly sleep in my foot,
Put it in the grey dog;
    The grey dog went through the townland
To seek milk for my foot.

Then the boy or girl who had the "prickly sleep" in his or her foot tramped, tramped, in imitation of the grey dog tramping through the townland in search of milk for the sleepy foot![13]

A combination of the banishing and transferring spell with what might be called the dwindling spell is illustrated by the Anglo-Saxon *Charm against Wens*:

> Wen, wen, little wen,
> here you shall not build, nor have any habitation,
> but you shall go north, hence to the neighbouring hill,
> where you wretch have a brother.
> He shall lay a leaf on your head;
> Under the wolf's paw, under the eagle's feather,
> under the eagle's claw, ever may you wither.
> May you be consumed as coal upon the hearth,
> may you shrink as dung upon a wall,
> and may you dry up as water in a pail.
> May you become as small as a linseed grain,
> and much smaller than the hipbone of an itchmite,
> and may you become so small that you become nothing.[14]

Another dwindling spell, which, the Anglo-Saxon manuscript says, "will be a remedy for you against a furuncle and scrofula and worms and every kind of evil," goes:

> In the case in hand nine spirits are supposed to have taken up their abode in the sore spot, and the charm undertakes to cure the patient by gradually reducing the number of spirits. The method employed is a favorite one in magic. One by one the spirits are driven out until ultimately none of them remains: the nine become eight and the eight seven and the seven six, and so on. The monotonous repetition of the same formula gives it an intensity and a weight that leaves no room for embellishments.

> Nine were Nothke's sisters.
> Then the nine became eight
> and the eight became seven

and the seven became six
and the six became five
and the five became four
and the four became three
and the three became two
and the two became one
and the one became none.

Sing *Benedicite* nine times.[15]

The number nine is a figure (or name) of power, being three times
the three which the deep mind always appears to accept as a powerful pattern, as is shown by the sacred and mystical nines and threes
in almost all cultures. Storms comments upon the dwindling or
"counting out" method of healing as follows:

The method of counting out the disease is likewise employed
in a charm against fever which says that the formula must be
repeated nine times on the first day, eight times on the second
day, and so on until the ninth day, after which the fever has
disappeared. As pneumonia, e.g., takes nine days to reach its
crisis, the magician must have gained much glory when the
patient recovered.

The method remained no less popular when writing came to
be used as a magical possibility. The magic word *Abracadabra*
was sometimes written down in this way:

abracadabra
abracadabr
abracadab
abracada
abracad
abraca
abrac
abra
abr
ab
a

The following, written on a blank piece of paper, enveloped in linen and bound on the patient, serves against a flow of blood:

icucuma
cucuma
ucuma
cuma
uma
ma
a[16]

Dwindling spells are often used in conjunction with the gradual destruction of an object into which the vitality of the disease has been transferred. A tree may be called upon to do this service when its leaves begin to fall, or a candle may be burned; fire may also be used. This method is well-known as a method of causing life itself to dwindle, too; from the time of the Ancient Greeks to our own it has appeared in folk tale and literature. Transference of a disease or discomfort to an object is often accomplished by touch. An unlit candle, for example, can be pressed to the affected part and told by either a mental or verbal message to take or accept the disease, and then lit and allowed to burn itself out. A gypsy spell makes use of a knife in healing a child who has bumped its head. The blade of the knife is pressed to the swelling, and the following spell is said three or seven or nine times, after which the knife is stuck into the earth the same number of times.

Be thou, be thou, be thou weak
And very soon perish!
Go thou into the earth,
May I see thee never more!
Bring knives, knives
Give into the earth.[17]

This is psychosomatic curing. A person with sufficient abilities in psychic concentration can do it for himself or herself.

In manoeuvres such as this the object to be used must be instructed verbally to play its part, just as the Wise Women usually instructed the herbs they gathered to be effective. Indeed the "medicines" used by folk-healers are almost always commanded or implored to give of their best, and the patient is usually made aware that this has occurred even if he himself has not been present at that part of the spell-making. An eleventh-century Anglo-Saxon manuscript gives us the following combination of spell-making and medication:

Remember, Mugwort, what you made known,
What you arranged at the Great Proclamation.
You were called Una, the oldest of herbs,
you have power against three and against thirty,
you have power against poison and against infection,
you have power against the loathsome foe roving through
    the land.

And you, Plantain, mother of herbs,
open from the east, mighty inside.
Over you chariots creaked, over you queens rode,
over you brides cried out, over you bulls snorted.
You withstood all of them, you dashed against them.
May you likewise withstand poison and infection,
and the loathsome foe roving through the land.

"Stune" is the name of this herb, it grew on a stone,
it stands up against poison, it dashes against pain.
Unyielding it is called, it dashes against poison,
it drives out the hostile one, it casts out poison.
This is the herb that fought against the snake,
it has power against poison, it has power against infection,
it has power against the loathsome foe roving through the land.

Put to flight now, Venom-loather, the greater poisons,
        though you are the lesser,
you the mightier, conquer the lesser poisons, until he
        is cured of both.
Remember, Camomile, what you made known,
what you accomplished at Alorford,
that never a man should lose his life from infection,
after Camomile was prepared for his food.

This is the herb that is called "Wergulu."
A seal sent it across the sea-ridge,
a vexation to poison, a help to others.
It stands against pain, it dashes against poison,
it has power against three and against thirty,
against the hand of a fiend and against mighty devices,
against the spell of mean creatures.

There the Apple accomplished it against poison
that she (the loathsome serpent) would never dwell in the house.

Chervil and Fennel, two very mighty ones.
They were created by the wise Lord,
holy in heaven as He hung [on the cross];
He set and sent them to the seven worlds,
to the wretched and the fortunate, as a help to all.

These nine have power against nine poisons.
A worm came crawling, it killed nothing.
For Woden took nine glory-twigs,
he smote then the adder that it flew apart into nine parts.

Now these nine herbs have power against nine evil spirits,
against nine poisons and against nine infections:
Against the red poison, against the foul poison,
Against the white poison, against the purple poison,
against the yellow poison, against the green poison,
against the black poison, against the blue poison,
against the brown poison, against the crimson poison.
Against worm-blister, against water-blister,
against thorn-blister, against thistle-blister,
against ice-blister, against poison-blister.

If any poison comes flying from the east,
or any from the north, [or any from the south],
or any from the west among the people.

Christ stood over diseases of every kind.

I alone know a running stream,
and the nine adders beware of it.
May all the weeds spring up from their roots,
the seas slip apart, all salt water,
when I blow this poison from you.

Mugwort, plantain open from the east, lamb's cress, venom-
loather, camomile, nettle, crab-apple, chervil and fennel, old
soap; pound the herbs to a powder, mix them with the soap and
juice of the apple. Then prepare a paste of water and of ashes,
take fennel, boil it with the paste and wash it with a beaten egg
when you apply the salve, both before and after.

Sing this charm three times on each of the herbs before you
(he) prepare them, and likewise on the apple. And sing the same
charm into the mouth of the man and into both his ears, and
on the wound, before you (he) apply the salve.[18]

The majority of traditional charms are directed to the dismissing
of the obvious symptoms or consequences of the disease. A typical
attack upon the symptoms of the disease of the "rose" in cattle
is the following from the gaelic.

Thou rose deathly, deadly, swollen,
Leave the udder of the white-footed cow,
Leave the udder of the spotted cow,
Leave, leave that swelling,
    And betake thyself to other swelling.

Thou rose thrawn, obstinate,
Surly in the udder of the cow,
Leave thou the swelling and the udder,
Flee to the bottom of the stone.

I place the rose to the stone,
I place the stone to the earth,
I place milk in the udder,
I place substance in the kidney.[19]

As I have said earlier, the curing or alleviating of symptoms is not always enough. Consequently, so far as it is possible to tell, it seems that while traditional spell-makers of old had considerable success in curing skin blemishes, warts, boils, sprains, and minor disorders in which what is obviously wrong is actually also either the whole of the disorder or nearly so, they had less success with major disease. Nevertheless there are many instances of serious illnesses being cured by spell-makers and faith-healers in the twentieth century. Dr. Alexis Carrell wrote:

> The most important cases of miraculous healing have been recorded by the Medical Bureau of Lourdes. Our present conception of the influence of prayer upon pathological lesions is based upon the observation of patients who have been cured almost instantaneously of various affections, such as peritoneal tuberculosis, cold abscesses, osteitis, suppurating wounds, lupus, cancer, etc. The process of healing changes little from one individual to another. Often, an acute pain. Then a sudden sensation of being cured. In a few seconds, a few minutes, at the most a few hours, wounds are cicatrised, pathological symptoms disappear, appetite returns. Sometimes functional disorders vanish before the anatomical lesions are repaired. The skeletal deformations of Pott's disease, the cancerous glands, may still persist two or three days after the healing of the main lesions. The miracle is chiefly characterised by an extreme acceleration of the processes of organic repair. There is no doubt that the rate of cicatrisation of the anatomical defects is much greater than the normal one. The only condition indispensable to the occurrence of the phenomenon is prayer. But there is no need for the patient himself to pray, or even to have any religious faith. It is sufficient that some one around him be in a state of prayer.[20]

The literature about faith healing either within or outside a particular religious faith is huge, and we must not attempt to summarize even a part of it here. It is, however, worth noting that Carrel speaks of the "state of prayer" and thus suggests that there is a special "state" in which messages of healing can be transmitted. Many people have explored the nature of this state and the nature of healing by "faith" or by "magic." In his book *The Medium, The Mystic, and the Physicist*, Lawrence Leshan identified two main healing methods, as a consequence both of studying the work of many noted healers including Olga and Ambrose Warral, Harry Edwards, Rebecca Beard, Agnes Sanford, Edgar Jackson, The Christian Science group, Parahantam Yogananda, Stewart Grayson, and Katherine Kuhlmann. He came to the conclusion that there were two types of healing.

In Type 1 healing, the healer goes into an altered state of consciousness in which he views himself and the healee as one entity. There is no attempt to "do anything" to the healee, but simply to meet him, to be one with him, to unite with him.

The healer views the healee in the Clairvoyant Reality at a level close to that in which All is One. However, he is focused by love, by caring, by *caritas*, on the healee. This is an essential factor.

It is essential that there be a deeply intense caring and a viewing of the healee and oneself as one, as being united in a universe – the Clairvoyant Reality – in which this unity is possible. "Become conscious for a single moment that Life and intelligence are ... neither in nor of matter [and] the body will cease to utter its complaints." So wrote Mary Baker Eddy.

The healers used a wide variety of "techniques" to attain this altered state of consciousness. Some prayed, some attempted to look at the healee from God's viewpoint or to see him as he looked from the spirit world, and some were able to describe what they did without much of an explanatory system. All agreed, however, that there must be intense caring and a viewing of the healee within a framework in which healer and healee could become one entity in a larger context without either of the two losing their individuality. Indeed, both would have their uniqueness enhanced by becoming one as do two people who fall in love.[21]

The second type of healing that Leshan identified concerns the use of energy flow from the hands. He states:

Type 2 is quite different from Type 1. The healer perceives a pattern of activity between his palms when his hands are "turned on" and facing each other. Some healers perceive this as a "flow of energy," some as a sphere of activity. The hands are so placed – one on each side of the healee's pathological area – so that this "flow of energy" is perceived to "pass through" the troubled area.

In Type 2 the healer *tries* to heal; he wants to and attempts to do so through the "healing flow." In both Type 1 and Type 2 he must (at least at the moment) care completely, but a fundamental difference is that in Type 1 he *unites* with the healee; in Type 2 he tries to cure him.[22]

Most spell-makers are aware of, and some use, both these types of healing, but there is for them a third. This is, of course, the verbally directed psychic message, which is quite precise and particular, and does not necessarily involve the total identification in a kind of psychic unity of the healer and subject as in Leshan's Type 1, and does not necessarily involve the use of energy by way of the hands as in Type 2. Sybil Leek in her book *Telepathy* refers to "psychic healing in the New Forest of England where telepathic communications were used to convey to a sick person that the body could be made healthy by vibrations coming from one mind to another." She also records:

Recently I went to the Yucatan Peninsula in search of a man I had met years ago, a witch doctor. I have always been eager to record incidents of witchcraft as they occur in the second half of the twentieth century. We had made a film of the events that led to visiting the witch doctor's straw hut several miles from Noona, a Mayan Indian village well off the beaten track of tourists, who think that Merida is typical of life in the Yucatan. We talked to many of the townspeople and learned that the witch doctor was held in high respect for his work, mainly in the realms of healing. I spent a lot of time talking to him and discussing herbs. He told me he used nothing but his mind and herbs in healing and indicated that he visualized the sick person as whole, then spent hours communicating this thought to the sick person. The testimony of the townspeople was that their witch doctor was "strong in mind" and they agreed that the percentage of his cures was satisfactory, which was good because there was no other medical aid and the town was so poor no one could have paid normal medical fees. I asked how much the witch doctor was paid and was told that everyone gave him food. Everyone I met said with pride that the witch doctor could "stop bleeding," a feat well known and used by many primitive people, including the gypsies of the New Forest. When questioned as to how this was done, there was rarely any difference in the replies from a dozen people. "He does it with his mind," they said, in complete acceptance of his powers.[23]

We are now, perhaps, nearing the heart of the matter, having noted that there seem to be two types of healing work, one which involves psychic messages without physical contact, and one which involves physical contact, and that in all cases there is a sense of "energy flow." This "energy flow" can be extremely exhausting for the transmitter of the message, especially if the disorder to be cured is a complicated or very serious one. Also, the patient may present some resistance for one reason or another. One type of resistance is caused by pain itself, so that it is necessary to get the pain out of the way before the message can "get through." Some spell-makers and healers "transfer" the pain to themselves—not the disease itself but the pain only—at the beginning of their operations and are then able to send the message effectively. This is often the case with spell-makers attending childbirth; they themselves suffer the labour pains, though not always for a very long time.

Healing spells, like all psychic healing operations, are dependent as much upon clarity of intent as upon the amount of psychic energy that can be transmitted. some times the explicit intent is not the same as the psychic desire and then things go awry. I came across an interesting case of this myself. The spell-maker was asked to write a spell to charm away a wart on the hand of a young boy unknown to her. The request was made more as a test of her powers, or of such spells in general, than as a wholehearted appeal for help. The spell ran:

151

Moon change child
change child
hands clear as moon
clean as moon
the skin is whole
the skin is clean
this palm
is healing itself
this hand is healing
this boy is healing himself
his hands grow clear
and stay clear
moon guards his fine hands
all her turning.[24]

The spell-maker set a time for the spell to work, a particular day, and on that day the first wart was joined by a second. There is an obvious explanation. The spell-maker had been asked to prove something and inwardly resented the challenge. Consequently, quite without conscious intention, she placed contraries in the spell, for if there is one thing obvious to us it is that the moon is *not* "clear" or "clean." It is, we know, pocked and pitted—in a word, warted. We can see shadows upon it from earth, and we have seen photographs of its surface many times. Thus the spell-maker used an image—the moon is for many spell-makers a name of power—which placed a contrary impulse in the spell. This alone, without her inner resentment, might not have had much effect, but the combination of a contrary image and a contrary feeling was enough to cause error.

In some instances, one healing spell is not enough. The spell-maker finds it necessary to make several, which may amount to a full course of treatment. He may begin with a preparatory spell, which gets the patient in a receptive condition, and then continue to tackle the illness in a series of spells, each one dealing with a further aspect of the disorder.

Here is another contemporary spell which is in three parts. It is close to being a prayer. It was written to cure a man hospitalized with an undiagnosed disorder that caused continual vomiting and the passing of blood anally. The man was in great fear of a stomach cancer or something equally serious, and was in very low spirits. Two days after the spell was written he left the hospital and, after some days of a carefully light diet, was pronounced entirely well; the disorder was stated to have been caused by some kind of poisoning. Because of the patient's state of mind the spell began with a call for peace and ease:

> Goddess, bring this spirit peace
> Bring it housing of good flesh
> Goddess, bring this spirit ease
>
> Goddess, bring all curing growth
> bring all strength and comfort, bring
> all ease of flesh, all ease of soul
> Goddess bring this man your healing
>
> Goddess, heal him in and out
> and through and round and every way
> Goddess make his eating good
> make his limbs be strong to strain
>
> Goddess, bring him every whole
> and holy comfort, every strong
> and easeful thing that man can have
> Goddess let his years be long
>
> his comfort sure his heart secure
> Goddess ease him ease him bring him peace
> Goddess heal make whole his heart
> and purify all that he is

This is a very direct, though generalized spell, using largely abstract terminology. It was, indeed, a preparatory cleansing spell, and was followed immediately by a more specific one:

> Let the soft belly become warm
> with firm comfort,

the bowel stir in certainty
his heart unharmed,
the body heal itself
with love

Goddess be the bearer of
this message to him: heal! Heal!
Cure thyself and cure thyself.
Goddess give him now the real

inward knowledge; let him have
the understanding of his way
and of his need and so be healed.
Goddess bring him every way

of peace and ease and strength that is
and make this message in his blood:
heal! heal! Goddess give
this man all there is of good

Here the spell-maker is dealing with the possibility that the physical disorder may be linked to psychological disorder, to anxieties and frustrations. The last spell of the series of three in this particular operation was simple, direct, and commanding:

Let the blood
and the gut
   be clean

Be whole   Be whole
   Heal   Heal[25]

Though this three-spell sequence is fairly abstract it is typical of many spells in its three-part structure. Often, as we have seen in looking at other spells, the whole is composed of three or more parts and rises by degrees to its final command, which may be very direct indeed. It is at this point that the spell-maker most usually feels a great surge of energy, and knows that "virtue" has gone out of him. The psychological concern of this spell is important. Just as pain can block out the receiving of a message, so can fear, anxiety, and guilt. Jesus Christ showed us the way when he began some of his healings with the words "Thy sins be forgiven thee." Having removed the block of guilt he could then send his psychic command and know it would be heard and obeyed.

Another spell in several parts is one to cure a child of earache, caused probably by sinus trouble. Here the language is less abstract, more image-laden.

I
Please, Dear Lady,
give to this
my child all comfort
and all ease;
cleanse her hearing,
free her breath
give her strength
and love and health

II
Let the ear be whole
and the calm seas
live in the movements
of her breath;
let the ear be healed
and the great winds
move softly
in all her moves;
let the ear be healed
let the ear be healed
let the ear be healed
and good sleep bring dawn
of happiness
of health
of calm
let the ear be healed
and sleep please dawn

III
To the brow coolth;
to the ear ease;
to the face calm;
to the mind peace[26]

The spell was written on Christmas Eve. The child was well enough to enjoy Christmas Day, the earache gone.

Both these spells were from the same hand, as can perhaps be detected from certain similarities of style. This spell-maker believes (and he is clearly here at one with the practitioners of Type 1 faith healing as described by Lawrence Leshan), that the healing message must include messages to the mind and spirit, blessings upon the mind and spirit of the person afflicted. An even simpler example of the way in which the healing spell inevitably includes spiritual attempts to heal the psyche as well as the body of the subject is the following part of a spell series against glaucoma:

Eyes be eased
Eyes be pure
Eyes be clear
And eyes be sure
Eyes be whole
Oh, Eyes be whole
And Eyes be light
Unto the Soul[27]

This rhymed spell is extremely traditional. It must be emphasized however, that rhymes are far from essential and that unless the spell-maker has a natural facility with rhyme it is best avoided, as hunting around for a rhyming word interrupts the concentration and the energy flow. Moreover the spell-maker may then be tempted not to write a spell but a poem, to make a literary artefact rather than a psychic message, in which case, of course, it will not work. One spell-maker I know who is also a poet finds that this happens very often and that the spell-making activity changes direction and becomes a poem-making activity. Spells may be poems by coincidence, by chance, but they are not required to be so. Here is an example of a spell delivered with enormous energy which has no poetic quality at all:

Be Whole
Be Whole
Be Whole
    Amen[28]

This, in its utter simplicity, approaches the non-verbalized message, and it should be emphasized here, perhaps, that some spell-makers do not use words, but simply send the message telepathically, visualizing the healing process, visualizing the event. Obviously one cannot include such non-verbal spells in a book of any kind; indeed, as they do not include words, they should not be called spells at all, though I do not know of another word with which to label them. Nevertheless, their existence emphasizes for us yet again that it is not the words as such which are the power of the spell, but the energy-flow that is transmitted within the message that the words guide to the correct destination.

8

Ways and Means

"How do we do it? By developing our minds to a point where we see or feel no barriers of time and space, when the horizons become limitless. Then we are able to experience the conquest of self, and influence others."

Sybil Leek

As the foregoing chapters have shown, spell-makers vary considerably in the ways in which they give their spells direction and force. Some spell-makers use most elaborate rituals, and some none. Some use talismans and charms, some potions, and some dispense with props altogether. It is therefore hard to establish anything of a rule book, even a "rule-of-thumb" book, for spell-making. Nevertheless, it is possible to describe some ways and means which spell-makers have found effective, and to indicate some of the difficulties the spell-maker must overcome.

First of all, the spell-maker should ideally have a room in which he or she can be alone, and which is not normally used by other members of the household. If this room is in constant use by others it retains traces of others' emotional lives and makes concentration difficult. Moreover, a room which contains pictures or objects which have strong associations that have nothing to do with the life of the spirit, with emotion and with meditation, can be an alien atmosphere in which to make spells. This is not to say that a spell-maker *must* have such a room; a practiced spell-maker can operate almost anywhere he or she is alone and free from interruption, whether it is a rumpus room or a kitchen or a motel room, but any sensible person would prefer to work in a sympathetic atmosphere. Some people create this atmosphere in terms of utter simplicity, using a room that is sparsely furnished, with bare white walls, the only objects being one or two which they associate with magic. Others festoon their walls with paintings that "feel right," fill the bookshelves with books about magic, mythology, and religion, and books of paintings and poetry, and crowd the various surfaces with pebbles picked up on beaches, small *objets d'art*, and plants. Yet others intensify the atmosphere of the room by including within it images which allude specifically to magic. They have three- or seven-branched candlesticks, wine goblets, astrological symbols, and so forth. The only rule is that what feels right *is* right, whether it makes sense to anybody else or not.

Entering this room with the firm intention of making a spell, the spell-maker must feel assured that he or she is properly prepared for the job. There are many different ways of giving oneself this assurance. Some people bathe before making a spell, saying to themselves, as they stand under the shower or lie in the bath, that they are cleansing both body and spirit. This does not work for everyone. Some find that the act of bathing relaxes them in the wrong way and makes them lethargic, or that the necessary towelling and scrubbing makes them too aware of their bodies and thus provides an obstruction rather than an aid to psychic activity. Some, bathed or not, choose to put on a particular piece of clothing, which is only worn when making spells. A favourite is, understandably, a simple white shift or a garment made of natural materials—wool, cotton, or linen. Some people wear a carefully chosen pendant around their necks, or a particular ring. Some like to work entirely naked. On the other hand, elaborate clothing interests some people. They like black clothes embroidered with symbols of the heavens or other traditional images of spiritual power. The beginner should, however, be warned that the more attention he or she pays to the creation of an effective environment and self-assuring clothing, the more self-conscious and therefore the less effective he or she is likely to be. Many would-be spell-makers and magicians spend too much energy on making the whole business entertaining to themselves. Indeed, I know a number of people who have a considerable stock of magical implements, images, and clothes, who could no more make a spell than I could sing opera. The important thing is to keep one's mind firmly upon the purpose of the spell and to perform it as simply, directly, and intensely as possible.

There is no end to the manoeuvres which you can try out in order to assist your concentration. Some believe that fasting for a period is important and useful, and for some people this may be the case. Some, on the other hand, find that one or two drinks beforehand can help them concentrate. Others find it useful to light candles and only pinch (never blow) them out when the spell is finished. Yet others burn incense. It is largely a matter of "whatever turns you on," and on the whole the less you need to turn you on the more efficient you are likely to be.

The attitude of the other people in the house is important. If they regard your activities as absurd, or if they are nervous or resentful, then you may have difficulties in overcoming the vibrations they emit. In such cases it is best to operate when you are alone in the house, or to ban everyone else from the room in which you work. If you can, however, you should manage to get your companions to accept your spell-making as a natural, ordinary, unremarkable activity. Don't talk about it incessantly, for this is bound to cause boredom and irritation in others. Don't make a big thing of it. You will find that far more people will accept it as a natural activity than you might suppose. In everybody there is still a child who believes in magic.

The time at which you make your spells is important. Most people make them in the evening or at night. This is partly because it's easier to concentrate when you know that the tensions of the day are all over and that you are not going to have to drop the whole thing in order to answer the phone or make a meal. It is also partly because at night your room is more enclosed, more private; the outside world is not disturbing you with birdsong, or traffic noise, or the chance glimpse of something moving outside your window. It is also because at night your whole body is gearing itself towards approaching sleep and dreams, to the increased activity of the subconscious mind. And finally, spell-making can be an exhausting activity and you may well wish to rest afterwards.

The actual spell-making activity can take many forms. Perhaps the best way to begin is by using one of the basic formulae which are illustrated in this book. Many of these are so constructed as to increase one's powers of transmission as the spell proceeds because their incantatory rhythms convince the maker of his or her power even as the power is being brought into use.

One of the easiest of these formulae is that based on the triad, which is to be found both in Gaelic and other spells and in ancient Celtic aphorisms. Let us assume that the spell is a blessing. One might then make a spell beginning:

Light in his mind
Calm in his heart
Strength in his hand
  Let this be.

Love in his house
Wisdom in his children
Wisdom in his ways
  Let this be.

As one composes a spell of this kind the spell can accumulate power if the concentration is kept up. If the concentration fails, so does the spell. In spells of this kind, in which qualities desired are being enumerated, it is wise to think out the general plan of the spell beforehand in order to be precise in language. This is especially true of the summoning spell used to bring a lover into one's life. Such a spell might begin:

You who are wise with the wisdom of the heart,
You who fill my heart with delight in your beauty,
You who understand all the ways of my mind,
  Come to me

Such summoning spells must always be worked out carefully, even exhaustively. One must be sure that the qualities listed are not in opposition to one another, and that *all* the really important qualities are there. It might be as well to include a reference to the marital situation of the desired person, not by saying "unmarried" (which is negative) but by saying in a more simple fashion "free to be mine" or something of that nature. The statements should all be positive. Summoning spells like this appear to work, possibly because the spell-maker, having completed the spell, is now psychically and intuitively as well as consciously on the alert and can therefore single the person out from the crowd. It may work also because in such spells there is always a reference to the desired one being attracted to the spell-maker, and this telepathic message can get across. The main problem with summoning spells is obvious. The more precise and detailed the spell, the more difficult it is to find the exact person, and therefore the longer it will take for the spell to work. One can, if one grows weary of waiting, produce a "booster shot," adding a less complicated spell on to the first one and indicating a time limit. When you are placing time conditions upon a spell, it is wise to look at a calendar and fix the time for the spell's fruition as the time of the almost-full or full moon, for at the time of the full moon everyone's intuitive energy is at its peak and the psyche is prepared for possible up-heaval and change. Some spell-makers only work when the moon is waxing or at the full, and never when it is on the wane. Others, of course, disregard the moon entirely, and simply make the spells when they feel they can and must, regardless of the calendar.

In mentioning this aspect of timing, I should also add that many spell-makers use astrology to determine the most propitious time to make the spell they wish. Again, this is a matter for the indi-vidual to decide. If one's belief in astrology is strong, then the use of astrology will reinforce the spell. If one's belief is weak or one's grip on astrology uncertain then there may be little point in using it, for one may find oneself growing self-conscious and aware of clumsiness. Working with the moon, however, is simpler. One has only to glance at a calendar or look up at the sky, and there are no complications to clutter one's mind, whereas astrological calculations can be very elaborate indeed.

Most spell-makers are interested to some extent in other aspects of magic and in some forms of divination. I do not myself believe that a spell-maker needs to study these other arts, but it is certainly good exercise for the intuitive "muscles" to work with the Tarot, or the *I Ching*, or any other "occult" system one finds sympathetic. But beware of becoming so fascinated with the elaborate and complicated symbolism of such systems as to inhibit yourself. A spell-maker who has to consult the Tarot by means of a full reading before making a spell is likely to develop a block and become incapable of transmitting psychic energy with the necessary unselfconscious simplicity and direct force.

There are many difficulties attendant on the use of elaborate rituals, surrounding one's spell-making with symbolic objects and qualifying it with esoteric knowledge. The spell-maker who works with talismans or with herbs and roots and with potions made from them can sometimes rely too heavily upon the physical objects and suppose them to have the power in themselves, whereas the power is all in the intent, in the psychic energy they are made to reinforce. Beginning spell-makers are liable also to create alibis for themselves by blaming the plants for their failure. Moreover, some recipes for gathering and mixing the plants are so complicated that any normal person is liable to feel uncertain as to whether the job has been done correctly. Thus from the very start, the effectiveness of the spell is likely to be undermined by doubts. Simplicity and directness are always best.

The actual making of the spell is difficult to describe clearly. I have over and over again used the words "intent," "concentration," and "energy," and we have considered the sensations felt by the spell-maker and have explored to some degree the nature of the process. But how can one learn to get into the right state to make spells?

Let us start by realizing that we all make use of telepathic messages in our daily lives. We have all sent messages to friends and loved ones across crowded rooms, without using words or even gestures; a meeting of the eyes—sometimes not even that—has been sufficient. We have all, seeing someone of the opposite sex who attracted us, sent out wordless messages of invitation, and have sometimes received answering messages of the same kind. Many of us have experienced a sense of instant communication with a stranger, have felt that he or she has been known to us before, or is in some way part of our own psychic "family." The beginning spell-maker should recall these occasions and the psychic sensations that accompanied them, and then try to use that part of the psyche which was used at those times. In this way he or she can learn to enter the message-sending state.

Once this state has been recreated, by making use of memory, it becomes fairly easy to enter it at will, provided always that the environment is not totally unsympathetic. If this state is entered with a passionate intent to send a specific message, then the spell-making itself is already begun. In this state, the spell-maker should visualize clearly the subject of the spell, and the more clearly one can visualize the subject the stronger the spell will be. It is, consequently, much easier to make spells which involve people you know well than people whom you have difficulty in recalling precisely to mind. If the spell is a healing spell, one must visualize the person first and then "zoom in" on the part of the body which needs attention. Sometimes this may be difficult, in that few of us save surgeons have much of an idea what the heart (let us say) actually looks like. In such cases, however, one's own visualization of a symbolic heart is quite effective. Different spells obviously require different degrees of visual precision.

Having visualized the subject, and having already, before the verbal shaping of the spell, sent out one's passionate message, one must then make the spell itself. Some spell-makers simply say it aloud, standing with their eyes closed and concentrating their energies. Some do not speak it aloud but only inside themselves, or only shape the words without giving them breath. Many, of course, write or type the spell. If you write the spell it should be on a clean piece of paper, and that piece of paper should be handled very carefully. Ideally you should write the spell without pause and without alteration, keeping up the concentration, until at the close you know the energy has been spent and that "virtue" has gone out of you. Sometimes, however, this proves impossible, and the written spell contains alteration and cancellations. In this case the manuscript can be used for a perfected reading aloud of the spell which will have no hesitations in it. You can always tell whether or not the hesitations have had any effect on the spell, for if they have broken the energy flow you will not, at the spell's end, feel that sense of energy spent, that sense of achieved commitment, which is quite unmistakable. The paper on which the spell is typed or written must now be looked after properly. It must be put in a place where it is by itself, not with other papers or objects, until you are certain that it has worked. Some people keep a desk-drawer empty for this purpose. Some use special boxes. The receptacle does not matter much; the one which seems good to you will be the right one. The spell should be put away immediately it has been made, and should not be looked at again until it has worked or until you are sure that it isn't going to work. A long-term spell can, of course, be brought out and read again as a "booster shot." It should not, however, be brought out for curiosity or for any reason other than reinforcing its power. If one makes several spells in a session, then each one should have a separate lodging place, unless all the spells are part of one operation or to do with the same subject.

I have stated all this rather dogmatically because many people destroy their own spells by carelessness. One cannot always tell how long it will take for a message to get through. A healing spell might act almost instantaneously or might take a week or more. Therefore, just to be on the safe side, do not assume too readily that a spell has completed its working, even though it appears to have been successful. Destroying the spell or placing it with other papers could qualify its effectiveness. This is based upon the belief that although one may know a spell has been completed, the message of the spell can continue to be sent without your being aware of it over quite a period. The spell-maker does, in fact, quite unconsciously continue to reinforce the message in small ways, by thinking of the subject of it, after the spell itself has been done.

Not every spell-maker works exactly in the way I have described. Some burn their spells after completion, feeling that the flames themselves reinforce the message and assure its success. Some place it in the house of the subject or bury it under the subject's threshold or put it in some other place they feel suitable. Some, of course, work in terms of gifts of amulets or other objects which are made to carry the message or reinforce it. As with other aspects of spell-making, the rule is that whatever you instinctively feel is right will be right. Moreover, different methods may be necessary for different kinds of spell.

The person beginning spell-making is likely to be initially somewhat uncertain of his or her abilities and even of the power of spells themselves. Many spell-makers have, indeed, begun with scepticism. A Kwakiutl indian, Quesalid, whose story is recorded in Franz Boas's *The Religion of the Kwakiutl*, began his career as shaman by joining a local group of shamans in order to expose their trickeries. He discovered that they used to conceal a piece of down in their mouths, and then, by biting their tongues or making their gums bleed, cover it with blood and then spit it out into the palm of the hand, informing the patient that here was the disease which had been removed. Scornful of this cheap trick, he nevertheless practised it and found that it actually worked. He gained a reputation as a master shaman with the shamans of a neighbouring tribe who used no down or blood but only spittle, and was able to cure people who remained unaffected by the spittle method. He went on to learn other tricks and to practise them, and eventually became a conscientious shaman, and appeared to have forgotten entirely his original intention of exposing shamanistic trickery. Indeed, he seemed to accept the trickery as symbolic, as an "outward and physical sign" of a spiritual act, a magical change. He also appeared to have understood that the power of suggestion is enormous and that tricks which intensify that power are not without validity; they are means to an end. Thus the Kwakiutl shaman took the same attitude as many Catholic priests who have tolerated and even invented "miraculous" happenings because such miracles increase the faith of their flocks.

This story is relevant to the beginning spell-maker, because it shows how it is possible to utilize the belief of others while remaining sceptical oneself. One can, indeed, sometimes cause a healing not by actually performing a spell, but by informing the subject of one's intention to perform the spell, or even by implying that a spell has been made when it has not. This may not be ethical, but there are times when the spell-maker simply cannot achieve the required state of mind to make a spell. In such cases he is in effect presenting the subject with a placebo, or perhaps relying more upon a bedside manner to set the patient on the way to recovery than upon actual medication.

I mention this aspect of spell-making here because it is important for the beginning spell-maker to realize that faith on the part of the subject may in some instances account for the success of a spell more than anything else, and that wherever possible this faith should be encouraged. Nevertheless the use of cheap tricks is to be avoided in general, for it undermines the spell-maker's own confidence in himself and in true magical power.

The beginner with little faith in his or her powers should adopt an attitude of mind that does not obstruct whatever energies can be transmitted. Say firmly to yourself, "Whether or not this spell will work, there is no earthly reason against attempting it. If it does work, then so much the better. If it doesn't, then nothing has been lost but a little of my time and energy, and, after all, I do strongly wish this thing to happen." Having said this, you can then make the spell without hesitation, and if it has been made both carefully and with concentration, it is likely to work.

Once the beginner has made a number of successful spells he or she faces a number of temptations. The first is the obvious temptation to use the skill for self-aggrandizement, to boast about it, to dramatize, to become conceited. If this temptation is not resisted you may soon find that you are making most of your spells with the intention of self-glorification, and that the intent to increase your own reputation as a spell-maker becomes stronger than the particular intent of any specific spell. Predictably, this causes the spell to fail. You are then tempted to resort entirely to tricks, and the effectiveness of your spells becomes totally dependent on the faith of the subject. In this way, the spell-maker becomes the magical equivalent of a quack doctor.

The second temptation is similar to the first. The successful spell-maker is liable to enjoy the sense of power for its own sake, to revel in it. As a consequence he or she may begin to use the power indiscriminately, carelessly, and crudely. The successful spell-maker must learn early on in his or her career that it is often as important to forego the power as it is to use it. This is especially the case when one is tempted to use binding and bidding spells, or curses and banishing spells, for such are always liable to reinforce the mortality-drive rather than the creative-drive in oneself, and lead to trouble and sickness. When contemplating the making of a spell, always ask yourself, "Is it a creative thing to do: does it enhance the quality of human life in any way?" Another question which must always be asked when the spell may cause discomfort to anyone is, "Is it absolutely necessary? Is there any other way of improving the situation?" It may be that the answers are "Yes" and "No" respectively, in which case you may find yourself possessed by a sense of moral obligation to make the spell which will improve people's lives at the cost of discomfort or pain to a single person or group. The White Witch Covens of England felt it a moral obligation to use their powers towards the destruction of Adolf Hitler, though they concentrated more upon the creation of a protective cone of power around England than upon actually destroying the Dictator.

As a spell-maker you must exercise self-discipline, and be very careful in your spell-making activities if the power is not to be lost or lead to self-destruction. The wise spell-maker will not make great claims for his or her power. Most spell-makers today keep their activities fairly quiet; they no longer need to hide themselves from the law in most Western countries, but they do feel that they should keep a low profile. Of course, there are exceptions, and there is no reason why anyone should not publicly admit their spell-making activities if they feel like it and are assured that they can cope with the consequences. These consequences can, of course, be tiresome and sometimes upsetting, as when one is asked to perform a healing spell upon a person with whom one can establish no telepathic connection, or when one is asked to "perform" as if one were some kind of entertainer. The spell-maker must always be prepared to make it clear on all occasions that he or she cannot make spells to order and that there are times when spells cannot be made. There are people one simply cannot get to; there are problems one cannot solve. No spell-maker can be effective on all occasions, though the practised spell-maker will be effective in nine out of ten cases where he or she feels that use of the power is possible.

Sometimes a spell may be effective and yet miscarry because the spell-maker has visualized the desired result incorrectly. I know of one instance when a spell-maker was called from his dinner by an agitated person who wanted him to make a spell to protect her and her husband and child on a plane flight they were about to make in a couple of days. The spell-maker thought it possible and forthwith made the spell, asking for calm skies, still clouds, and so forth. Unfortunately, however, he visualized the calm sky from the viewpoint of the ground and said nothing about travelling through the sky at all. Two days later his friend decided to cancel the trip. The spell had grounded her. The difficulty of correct and precise visualization is one that all spell-makers face over and over again.

One difficulty peculiar to makers of purely verbal spells is caused by their general appreciation of poetry. Much poetry contains spell-like elements and many spells have great poetic force. I mentioned earlier that the spell-maker who also writes poetry may find that he or she becomes more interested in the poetic than in the magical power of what is being written. I know one spell-maker who finds this a perpetual difficulty. In order to solve this problem it is necessary to perceive the differences between the spell and the poem. There are several. Firstly, the poem ususally contains images and statements which, while increasing the emotional effect of the structure, do not contribute directly to the precision of the command, but rather weaken it by elaboration.

Thus we might find a spell-maker saying:

> Bless this girl with the peace
> of the full round moon that shines
> on the still waters of the bay.

Here, while the image of the "full round moon" is vivid and the phrase "the still waters of the bay" adds to the feeling of peace which the spell gives, the elaboration weakens the message. It would be better if it read, more directly and simply:

Bless this girl with the peace
Of the moon on still waters

On the whole the shorter the spell the more effective it will be. The elaborately poetical spell can also distract the mind of the speaker from the spell's main intention. The general rule, therefore, is to keep it snappy, or at least not to attempt long spells until one is sufficiently experienced to cope with the extended effort they demand.

Sometimes the spell-maker who is also interested in the making of poetry will include references and images which do not carry conviction to the deep mind. These may fail because they are too particular; a spell-maker might use the image of a cat because he has himself a gentle and affectionate tabby. Thinking of this particular cat he might say:

Let her share the peace of the cat.

Unfortunately not all cats are peaceful, and the deep mind is likely to receive a confused message, or even to think of the "peace" of the cat as the peace which comes after a hunting trip and meal of meat. The deep mind is reluctant to accept messages which are phrased in terms of particular individual experience. It prefers long-tested symbols. Thus though our present experience of a queen may be of seeing a pleasant middle-aged woman smiling from the back seat of an open car, the deep mind is likely to accept the word as having all the awesome power of Queens of myth and legend. The spell-maker who also makes poems may be tempted to put a picture of a definite queen in his spell and thus weaken the message. It cannot be too often stated that while the spell must be made in words that have powerful emotional connotations for the speaker it must also be made in words that appeal to the speaker's deep mind and that also make sense to the deep mind of the person to whom the message is being sent.

The poem also differs from the spell in presenting more than one emotional tone, in presenting human complexities which involve hesitation, doubt, and counter-statement. Indeed, the greatest poems, however short, usually include elements of debate and of intellectual discussion which would cause a spell to fail. On the other hand, the spell which is so powerful in its language as to command immediate attention from the reader, and which is dominated by an emotional need with which most readers can immediately sympathize, will be accepted as poetry as well as magic.

Even here, however, there are few certainties, for poetry itself does send messages to the deep mind of its readers and does persuade people and therefore change them. Consequently a great poem, however much it breaks the rules of the spell, may have magical power, just as music, dance, and all forms of art can have this power to different degrees for different people. The person overwhelmed by a symphony or a painting, however, is usually not directed to perform any specific action or change in any specific way; the effect is general, however tremendous it may be. Nevertheless, some spell-makers are able to utilize existing poems and pieces of music as spells by performing them with magical intent.

Here we arrive at the heart of the matter, and I find myself saying again, "The intent is all." The spell is a vehicle for the intent. It is a means, an implement, and not, in itself, a power. Alexandra David-Neel in her fascinating book, *Magic & Mystery in Tibet*, tells a story which illustrates the way in which an effective magical implement may be made out of what seems distinctly unpromising material, and quotes a Tibetan proverb which sums up a great deal of what I have been saying.

The aged mother of a trader who went each year to India, asked her son to bring her a relic from the Holy Land. The trader promised to do so, but his mind being much occupied with the cares of his business, he forgot his promise.

The old woman felt very sad, and the next year, when her son's caravan started again, she renewed her request for the holy relic.

Again the trader promised to bring one, and again he forgot it. The same thing happened for the third time the following year. However, this time the merchant remembered his promise before reaching his home and was much troubled at the idea of

172

once more disappointing his aged mother's eager expectation.

As he pondered over the matter, seeking a way to mend his neglect, he caught sight of a piece of a dog's jaw lying near the road.

A sudden inspiration came to him. He broke off a tooth of the bleached jaw-bone, wiped away the earth which covered it and wrapped it in a piece of silk. Then, having reached his house, he offered the old bone to his mother, declaring that it was a most precious relic, a tooth of the great Sariputra.

Overjoyed, her heart filled with veneration, the good woman placed the tooth in a casket on the altar of the family shrine. Each day she worshipped before it, lighting lamps and burning incense. Other devotees joined in the worship and after a time rays of light shone from the dog's tooth, promoted holy relic.

A popular Tibetan saying is born from that story:

> "*Mos gus yod na*
> *Khyi so od tung.*"

Which means, "If there is veneration even a dog's tooth emits light."[1]

Sarah Lyddon Morrison makes a similar point in *The Modern Witch's Spellbook*, when she says:

No matter how complex or simple the ritual, the force that makes a magic spell work is the same in all cases. Nine days of fasting, little sleep, and the intoxicating fumes of narcotic herbs burning on an altar may produce a devil to do your bidding, but overwhelming emotion conjured in a few minutes of concentrated hatred, love, or avarice can also create desired results. For the power of magic is in the force of an emotion directed at a person or object.[2]

She continues to say:

The key, of course, is that not just any old emotion will do. There are degrees of feeling, and in magic, only the highest pitch of emotion has any effect whatsoever. Part of being a witch, classic or not, is developing an ability to arouse an enormous quantity of feeling, and it takes super-human concentration to summon and project it properly. It's also perfectly useless to aspire to become a witch without the ability to form clear mental images in the mind's eye. Many people, regrettably, don't think in pictures, but rather in words, and so are unable to create a photograph-perfect image of the person they wish to bewitch. It's essential to be able to focus mentally on the subject while at the same time casting powerful thought-waves of emotion at him.

What magicians do, really, is to will waves of hatred or love at a person by telepathy, for lack of a better word. More and more is being learned about the effects of strongly projected feelings – notably on plants, which react perceptibly to both human love and human hatred. Science fiction tells us that eventually we will be able to communicate telepathically with each other, perhaps even to freeze an enemy in his tracks with a look. Magic, mankind's oldest religion, has always celebrated the power of the mind to control and alter relationships. Perhaps the concept of ancient magic will in the future govern every aspect of our lives.[3]

This last statement is somewhat excessive. It is useful, however, in that it points to another difficulty the spell-maker must face. This is the temptation to allow spell-making to become too important to one's daily life, to rely upon spells to the exclusion of common sense and practical considerations. If one does this one is liable to fall victim to "witchcraft thinking" and therefore to see the world as no more than a battleground for competing psyches. I am not suggesting that this may not be, in part, true. The world *is* a place where psychic energies are in continual conflict. It is also a place where psychic cooperation occurs, and where the collective will of communities and peoples operates both for good and ill. I do, however, believe that our psychic powers are no more than a part of us, though they are an important part. They are as important as our powers of ratiocination, as our appetites, and as our physical faculties. Man has many attributes, and the psychic ones are only parts of the whole. If one develops these attributes to the exclusion of others one may, possibly, become a mystic, a saint, a seer; one may also on the other hand become a lunatic or at least a neurotic, just as someone who develops his taste for good food and wine may become a gourmet or a glutton. Moreover, anyone who over-uses his or her spell-making capabilities is liable sooner or later to fall into a state of narcissistic self-delusion, to believe that this power makes him or her a special kind of person who can control and alter human beings and their affairs, and, moreover, do so with increasing wisdom. It cannot be too strongly stated that the ability to make spells does not carry with it the ability to make them wisely. The spell-maker is not necessarily a wise person; he or she may well be in many respects a fool or a knave. The fool and the knave, however, are unlikely to last long as spell-makers, for their follies and their machinations will sooner or later lead them into the making of spells which will either backfire on them or get them into difficulties. Anyone who turns to the making of spells must do so without desire for self-aggrandizement, without hunger after power for its own sake, and without conceit or pretension. Anyone who turns to spell-making in this way, and with compassion for others and the desire to use his or her psychic energies to enhance the quality of life, will find that, while spell-making is not a mystic way or a path to spiritual illumination, it can result in a certain inner peace, for the maker of spells is rewarded by a feeling that he or she is making full and proper use of his or her emotional life and is no longer irritated by the continual repetition of that frustrating feeling that "There is nothing I can do about it." There is, for the spell-maker, always something that can be done about it.

Notes

Introduction

1. *In* George Barton Cutten: *Three Thousand Years of Mental Healing*, Scribners 1911, p. 5.
2. Paul Huson: *Mastering Witchcraft: A Practical Guide for Witches, Warlocks and Covens*, G. P. Putnam's Sons 1970, p. 24.
3. Ibid, p. 27.

Chapter One

1. Alexander Carmichael: *Carmina Gadelica*, Vol. IV (1941), p. 305.
2. Ibid, p. 309.

Chapter Two

1. N. K. Chadwick: *Poetry and Prophecy*, Cambridge University Press, 1942, p. 8.
2. Bronislaw Malinowski: *Coral Gardens and their Magic*, Allen & Unwin 1935, Vol. I, p. 147.
3. Ibid, pp. 143–144.
4. Richard Winstedt: *The Malay Magician*, Routledge & Kegan Paul 1951, p. 76.
5. Alexander Carmichael: op. cit., Vol. II (1900), p. 121.
6. John R. Seanton: *Religious Beliefs and Medical Practices of the Creek Indians*, 42nd Annual Report, Bureau of American Ethnology, Washington D.C., 1928, pp. 473–672.
7. *In* Samuel Allen: *Poems from Africa*, Thomas Y. Crowell Company 1973, p. 37. Translation by S. A. Babalola.

Chapter Three

1. Kuno Meyer (Trans.): *Selections from Ancient Irish Poetry*, Constable, pp. 25–26.
2. Alexander Carmichael: op. cit., Vol. II (1900), pp. 145–151.
3. Ibid, pp. 72–73.
4. C. M. Bowra: *Primitive Song*, Mentor Books 1962, p. 189. Translated from R. P. Trilles, *L'Ame du Pygmee d'Afrique*, Paris 1945, p. 424.
5. C. M. Bowra; op. cit., pp. 50–51, *from* Report of the Canadian Arctic Expedition 1913–18, Vol. XIV (1925) p. 459.
6. J. Frank Stimson: *Tuamotuan Religion*, Bishop Museum Bulletin No. 103, Honolulu 1933, pp. 32–33.
7. Jerome Rothenburg (Ed.): *Technicians of the Sacred*, Doubleday 1968, p. 359.
8. Ibid, p. 360.

Chapter Four

1. Ernest Rhys: *Fairy Gold*, J. M. Dent 1907, p. 1976.
2. Alexander Carmichael: op. cit., Vol. III (1940), p. 207.
3. Ibid., p. 165.
4. Ibid., p. 93.
5. Abragail and Valaria: *How To Become A Sensuous Witch*, Coronet 1971, p. 19.
6. F. Bruce Lamb: *Wizard of the Upper Amazon*, Houghton Mifflin 1975, pp. 32–33.
7. Ibid, pp. 89–90.
8. Alexander Carmichael: op. cit., Vol. III (1940), p. 241.
9. Ibid, Vol. IV (1941), p. 65.
10. Ibid, Vol. II (1900) p. 101.
11. C. M. Bowra: op. cit., p. 53. *Translated from* H. Vedder, *Die Bergdama*, 2 vols., Hamburg 1923, Vol. II, p. 63.
12. 39th Annual Report, Bureau of American Ethnology, Washington D.C. 1925.
13. Bronislaw Malinowski: op. cit., Vol. I, pp. 233–234.
14. C. M. Bowra: op. cit., p. 69.
15. Paul Huson: op. cit., p. 56.

16. Alexander Carmichael: op. cit., Vol. III (1940), p. 361.
17. William S. Baring-Gould: *The Annotated Mother Goose*, Bramhall House 1962, p. 226.
18. Ibid, p. 227.
19. Countess Evelyn Martinengo-Cesaresco: *Essays in the Study of Folk Songs*, Dent Everyman's Library Edition n.d., p. 164.
20. Ibid, p. 166. Translation by C. G. Leland.
21. Ibid., p. 243.
22. Ibid, pp. 247–248.
23. Lewis Spence: *The Fairy Tradition in Britain*, Rider and Company 1948, p. 166.
24. G. Storms: *Anglo-Saxon Magic*, Martinue Nijhoff 1948, pp. 209, 211.
25. Ibid, p. 209.
26. Ibid, p. 217.
27. Alexander Carmichael: op. cit., Volume II (1900), p. 57.
28. Anonymous: contemporary Canadian.
29. Maurice Bloomfield (Trans.): *Hymns of the Atharva-Veda*, OUP 1897, Motilal Banarsidass Edn., Delhi 1973, pp. 163, 473.

Chapter Five

1. Anonymous: contemporary Canadian.
2. Ruth Benedict: *Patterns of Culture* (1934), Mentor Books Edn. 1946, pp. 175–178.
3. Ian Hogbin: *A Guadalcanal Society*, Holt, Rinehart and Winston 1964, pp. 86–87.
4. Ibid, p. 87.
5. Ibid, p. 87.
6. C. G. Leland: *Gypsy Sorcery* (1891), Tower Books Edn. n.d., p. 127.
7. A. Grove Day: *The Sky Clears; Poetry of the American Indians*, University of Nebraska Press 1951, p. 80.
8. C. M. Bowra: op. cit., p. 149, *from* K. Rasmussen, The *Netsilik Eskimos*, Report of the 5th Thule Expedition, Copenhagen 1931, p. 279.
9. Ibid, p. 116.
10. A. Grove Day: op. cit., p. 109, *from* 39th Annual Report, Bureau of American Ethnology, Washington D.C. 1925.
11. Anonymous: contemporary.
12. Anonymous: contemporary.

13. Bloomfield: op. cit., pp. 106–7.
14. Bloomfield: op. cit., p. 107.
15. *In* Jerome Rothenburg (Ed.): *Shaking the Pumpkin*, Doubleday 1973, p. 48.

Chapter Six

1. Theodore Roethke: *Collected Poems*, Doubleday 1966, p. 217.
2. Bloomfield: op. cit., p. 102.
3. Bloomfield: op. cit., p. 104.
4. Bloomfield: op. cit., p. 104.
5. Paul Christian: *The History and Practice of Magic*, Citadel Press 1972, Vol. II, p. 412.
6. Verrier Elwin: *Folk Songs of Chattisgarh*, OUP 1946, p. 231.
7. Richard Winstedt: *The Malay Magician*, Routledge & Kegan Paul 1951, p. 149.
8. Ibid, p. 83.
9. Ibid, pp. 83–84.
10. Paul Huson: op. cit., p. 108.
11. C. G. Leland: op. cit., p. 128.
12. Paul Huson: op. cit., pp. 122–123.
13. Lenore Kandel: *The Love Book*, Stolen Paper Edn., San Francisco 1966, p. 4.
14. Edward Powys Mathers (Ed. and Trans.): *The Garden of Bright Waters: One Hundred and Twenty Love Poems*, Basil Blackwell 1920, p. 19.
15. Edward Powys Mathers: *Song to Shahryar: Poems from the Book of the Thousand Nights and One Night*, The Casanova Society 1925, p. 93.
16. Anonymous: contemporary.
17. Bloomfield: op. cit., pp. 31–32, 369.
18. Alexander Carmichael: op. cit., Vol. II (1900), p. 41.
19. Anonymous: contemporary.
20. Robert Graves: *The White Goddess*, Faber (1948), 1952 Edn., p. 202.
21. Anonymous: contemporary.
22. Rabindranath Tagore: *The Gardener*, Macmillan and Co. 1943, pp. 20–22.
23. Anonymous: contemporary.
24. Eric Maple: *Incantations and Words of Power*, Samuel Weiser, Inc., 1974, p. 21.
25. Ibid, p. 21.
26. Robin Skelton: *Because of Love*, McClelland and Stewart 1977, p. 41.

Chapter Seven

1. Alexander Carmichael: op. cit., Vol. II (1900), p. 19.
2. Siv Cedering Fox (Trans.) *in Antaeus 16*, Winter 1975, p. 83.
3. Ibid, p. 83.
4. C. G. Leland: op. cit., p. 65.
5. Thomas R. Breddle and Claude W. Unger: *Folk Medicine of the Pennsylvanian Germans* (1935), August M. Kelley 1970, p. 125.
6. Ibid, p. 67.
7. Anonymous: contemporary.
8. Breddle and Unger: op. cit., p. 67.
9. Alexander Carmichael: op. cit., Vol. IV (1941), pp. 242–243.
10. Ibid, Vol. IV (1941), p. 253.
11. C. G. Leland: op. cit., pp. 50–51.
12. Ibid, Vol. IV (1941), p. 257.
13. Ibid, Vol. IV (1941), p. 248.
14. G. Storms: op. cit., p. 155.
15. Ibid, pp. 150–151.
16. Ibid, p. 153.
17. C. G. Leland: op. cit., p. 89.
18. Ibid, pp. 187, 189, 191.
19. Alexander Carmichael: op. cit., Vol. II (1900), p. 7.
20. Alexis Carrel: *Man, The Unknown*, Hamish Hamilton 1935, p. 145.
21. Lawrence Leshan: *The Medium, The Mystic, and the Physicist*, The Viking Press 1974, pp. 106–108.
22. Ibid, pp. 112–113.
23. Sybil Leek: *Telepathy*, The Macmillan Company, New York, 1971, pp. 155–156.
24. Anonymous: contemporary.
25. Ibid.
26. Ibid.
27 Ibid.
28. Ibid.

Chapter Eight

1. Alexandra David-Neel: *Magic and Mystery in Tibet*, Penguin Books 1971, pp. 300–301.
2. Sarah Lyddon Morrison: *The Modern Witch's Spellbook*, Lyle Stuart 1971, p. 3.
3. Ibid, pp. 3–4.